`

First Edition

Edited by Lauren Roquemore

MIRACLES

God's amazing works in the life of one family

Duane Roquemore

This book was written for and is dedicated

to my three children: Lauren, Ryan and Hannah.

If they are the only three people who ever

read this book, it will have been well worth

the effort.

Preface

Wikipedia: "A miracle is an event attributed to divine intervention."

In 2011 I was going through a particularly difficult trial at work. Hardly an hour would go by without some reminder of the stressful situation I was enduring. In the midst of this trial I began to recall some of the amazing miracles God had performed in my life. I decided to write down as many as I could remember. It was quite a list. There were big miracles and small ones. It was a huge encouragement to me to remember all that God had done for me in the past. Writing them down helped me to endure the trial at work.

Also in 2011 my oldest daughter Lauren started high school. All of our friends with children in college told us the same thing; "High school will fly by so quickly! Those four years will be over before you know it!" To be honest this was pretty depressing. I can't imagine the day when I will have to say goodbye to my Lolo (Lauren) or any of my three kids. I am very close to all of them.

I began to think about my list of miracles and about my children leaving home one day. Although my wife Cathy and I had talked to our kids in a general way about the amazing things God had done in our lives, I wanted them to have a detailed account, something they could take with them when they left us. A book made the most sense to me. The problem was I had never written a book. Other than a million work e-mails and countless PowerPoint presentations, I had not written anything significant since college.

I sat around thinking "what a great idea" and then did nothing about it. God often sends us confirmation when an idea is truly from Him. At the time I had the idea for this book I was speaking at a small meeting for Global Media Outreach, a Christian organization where I do volunteer work. The topic had nothing to do with books or book writing; it was about internet based evangelism. After the meeting, a woman approached me and handed me a flyer for an organization for Christian writers. She invited me to come and speak at one of their events. My immediate thought was "Okay I think God might really want me to write this book." God certainly wasn't being very subtle.

In spite of this I still didn't get started for almost one year. My wife and I both work full-time and with three children, our lives are incredibly busy. I wasn't sure how I would ever find the time to get this done but, slowly, I found small pockets of time and began writing. I don't know if anyone other than my family and close friends will ever read this book. Quite honestly it's doesn't matter to me. I wrote this book for my three children. And I hope it will impact them in a significant and meaningful way. I hope that after they have left our home they will remember all of the times when God stepped into some very difficult situations and worked miracles. And I want them to remember that God is the same yesterday, today and forever. The same God who protected and blessed our family will do the same for them, if they let Him, if they make room for Him in their lives.

There is a theme for this book and it's found in Psalms 34:19: "Many are the afflictions of the righteous, but the Lord delivers him out of them all." Lauren, Ryan and Hannah, you live in a fallen world, a world scarred by sin, so you will be afflicted by difficulty and hardship throughout your lives. You know this already. You have been hurt by friends at school. You have been bullied and rejected. Although you can't avoid these trials, you can know that God will deliver you through each one. Every affliction will eventually come to an end. The Lord "will" deliver you!

ONE

War

I was born in Saigon, Vietnam at the height of the Vietnam War. I spent my first few weeks of life hiding in a bomb shelter at my grandparent's home. It wasn't only the war that threatened my life as an infant, it was an allergy.

I was a sickly child with severe milk allergies. My parents tried every possible infant formula to no avail. They all caused constant diarrhea and dehydration. I was malnourished and dying. Mom and dad took me to the hospital, expecting me to die there. The other three infants with whom I shared a crib all died. The doctors eventually found a new infant formula that my body accepted. I guess you could say I had a pretty rocky start in life!

I was the third of six children in a middle class family. My dual income parents were well educated and lived comfortably. Life was easy until the last few years of the war. America withdrew their troops from Vietnam in 1975. Mom and dad hated Communism and were concerned about the fate of South Vietnam. Our family didn't have a choice but to become refugees. We left everything behind and packed what would fit in a backpack: a change of clothing, family pictures and legal documents.

At the time the war ended, dad worked alongside CIA agents and high ranking military personnel. He had to leave Vietnam otherwise he would have been sent to a concentration camp or, worse, shot for treason.

Our family secretly left school one day and drove to the safety of the American Embassy. We waited until a military airplane was ready to transport Vietnamese civilians to America.

I have vivid memories of the cargo plane that we boarded on our flight out of Vietnam. As our plane taxied down the runway, women and children began crying and throwing up. The North Vietnamese Army was trying to shoot down our plane. They didn't want anyone to escape.

For the second time in my brief seven year life I thought I was going to die. Miraculously, our plane made it safely down the runway. My mom, my five siblings and I all managed to escape.

One of the most famous and iconic pictures of the Vietnam War is of a helicopter evacuating people from the roof of the American Embassy. My dad was there on that fateful day. People were fighting and pushing, trying to get into each helicopter that landed. One of my dad's bosses, a CIA agent, reached down into the chaos and pulled my dad onto a helicopter. He managed to escape, but at the time I didn't know if

I would ever see my dad again. He was reunited with us at a Marine Corp base in San Diego, California called Camp Pendleton.

My family was fortunate to evacuate by airplane. I have relatives who tried to escape on fishing boats that capsized, drowning everyone onboard. Other relatives were promised a flight out of Vietnam but were left behind. A plane similar to mine, full of women and children, crashed killing everyone onboard.

While at Camp Pendleton all of the refugee children attended school. Tents were set up to teach us English. I remember attending the final day of a catechism class. I didn't attend all of the sessions and didn't know any of the answers to the priest's questions about God. I didn't pass the test so I was surprised when the priest allowed me to come forward to take my first communion. I felt close to God that afternoon and my family told me I looked different. I was smiling widely and glowing from within. I didn't know what I was doing or what communion was about. But I felt God's presence that day.

A Catholic church in Oak Park, Illinois sponsored our family, agreeing to help us get established in America. They paid our rent and helped mom and dad find jobs. They helped us in so many ways; introduced us to public schools, taught us how to shop at grocery stores, showed us how to use laundromats and mass transit, and of course introduced us to McDonalds. We spent many holidays with our new American families. I will be forever grateful for their kindness and generosity. They were Heaven sent.

Mom and dad couldn't adjust to the extreme winters in Illinois, having previously lived in a tropical climate. When mom and dad heard of the many job opportunities and mild weather in California, they saved some money and borrowed more from my uncle to buy airfare to California for all eight of us. We moved from Oak Park, Illinois on my 9th birthday. The rest of my childhood was relatively uneventful and was spent in Hacienda Heights, a suburb in Southern California.

TWO

From Death to Life

My first memory of my dad was when I was around four years old. I was standing at the top of a staircase that led to the basement of our home in Southern California. I don't remember much about the home other than the basement. The stairs were steep and it was very dark down below. My dad was standing at the bottom of the stairs saying "Jump!" I honestly don't remember if I jumped but the experience was so traumatic that it became my earliest sustained memory in life.

It is fitting that my oldest memory of my dad would be so traumatic since this would become the pattern for our entire 41 years together. Until he passed away in September of 2006, my dad was the source of continual frustration and anger in my life.

My dad was born in 1930 in a tiny town in Southern Oklahoma named Roff. Even today Roff is a sad, ugly little town, barely a wide spot in the road. He grew up during the Great Depression with parents who showed him very little love. My grandmother was a Christian but I don't believe my grandfather was ever saved.

Although my grandparents remained married for more than 50 years, they fought almost constantly throughout their marriage. My dad grew up in a broken, dysfunctional family.

My dad had an older brother named Alvin, who died at the age of seven, and a younger sister named June. After Alvin died my grandparents, my dad and his sister made a never ending series of trips between Roff, Oklahoma and the west coast as my grandfather looked for work during the Depression.

My grandfather would find a job in California or Oregon, lose it, and then head back to Oklahoma to try farming again. I remember my aunt telling me about one of these return trips to Oklahoma. My grandmother was so depressed about having to return again to Oklahoma that she sat by their car somewhere in New Mexico crying her eyes out. The Great Depression was a miserable time for them.

My dad would leave home periodically during his high school years and live my with my Aunt Dorothy and Uncle Nelson on their huge cattle ranch in Cannon City, Colorado. This was his escape I guess. One time while living in Oregon my dad told his parents he was going to hitch-hike back to Colorado. My grandfather bought my dad a bus ticket and set him on his way. My dad was probably 16 at the time. There was one family story about how my dad was completely broke after leaving home for good.

Apparently my grandparents could have sent him money but refused.

My dad eventually settled in Los Angeles in the late 1940s and found a good paying job in the printing industry. He met my mom in Los Angeles. She was from a larger town in Oklahoma called Stillwell. She also had left Oklahoma for the west coast to find work. They were married in 1958 and raised their five children in a Southern California city called San Dimas. We grew up in a Brady Bunch type "house", but definitely not a Brandy Bunch type "home".

I don't understand why my dad ever bothered to have children. I am completely convinced that not only did he not love any of his five children; he also didn't love my mom. I have three children of my own and I absolutely love spending time with them. I cannot count the number of hours I've spent talking with them, playing catch with them and fishing with them. I wake them up every morning for school and tuck them in every night for bed. I try not to let more than a week go by without telling them that I love them. I'm not a perfect dad but I love my kids and pour myself into their lives.

My dad was the exact opposite of everything I've become as a dad. In the 41 years we shared together he never once told me that he loved me. He never once threw a ball with me. He never once had a meaningful conversation with me. Even though I was the only one of his five children to earn a bachelor's degree, he didn't give me one word of congratulation.

Worse than the things he "didn't" do were the things he "did" do. He never missed an opportunity to criticize me. Even when I tried to win his favor by doing something constructive he found something negative to say. For example, there was an unfinished project in the garage that was lingering for several months. I finished it without being asked and he found fault in my actions. I used my own money to dramatically improve the appearance of my room and his response was "he doesn't deserve a nice room like that."

Dad took us to Grace Baptist Church in Glendora, California three times a week: Sunday mornings, Sunday nights and Wednesday nights. My dad was a "religious" man, pious and proud. Later in life I found the right term for him: Pharisee. The Pharisees were some of the most "religious" people in Israel during the time of Christ. And they were completely lost.

This church we attended was what I call a "dead" church. It was filled with people like my dad. It was more of a social club than a church. Most of the people who attended were from upper middle class families. Because we were lower middle class we were never completely accepted by these people. There was an unspoken "cast" system that was firmly in place. This additional rejection by "religious" people gave me yet another reason to be angry with God.

So this was the environment in which I started my life. A dad who was outwardly "religious" but who had no love for me or our family. A dad who never spoke one word of encouragement, only criticism. A church filled with people just like my dad. A church that was spiritually "dead".

By the time I entered the 6th grade my broken relationship with my dad began to take its toll. I began to be filled with hate, anger and rage. These feelings were not just directed at my dad but also at God. I hated my dad and because he claimed to be a Christian I hated God as well. I remember how I would look up at the sky toward where I thought God might be, give Him the finger and direct every "four letter word" I could think of toward Him.

My best friend in sixth grade was Danny, the biggest drug addict in our school. I had a reputation for having the foulest mouth in middle school. I began smoking cigarettes in 6th grade, secretly of course. I was getting into fights at school, all the while attending church three times a week.

Things just got worse and worse as I progressed through middle school. I had an anger and hatred that were so strong they defy words. My mom, who was a wonderful Christian woman, saw what was happening to me and tried to reach out to me. She would write me notes and tape them to my bedroom door. I wouldn't read them and instead would shred them with my Marine Corp knife then tape them back onto the outside of my door. I'm sure I broke her heart a hundred times.

By the end of the 7th grade things were so bad that my parents pulled me out of public school and sent me to a small Christian school for 8th grade. They must have concluded that my downward spiral was related to bad influences at school when in fact my dad was the root cause.

They could not have picked a worse place to send me. It turned out that this tiny school was actually a school of last resort for kids who got kicked out of public schools. My 12 or so classmates were 10 times worse than the typical kids from my public school. Things got even worse. I got into more fights and I absolutely terrorized that school. The entire teaching staff turned over the year I was there. Academically I actually "lost" knowledge that year! The school was a mess. A perfect fit for me. My parents never said anything to me but must have suspected they had made a big mistake. They told me I'd return to public school for 9th grade.

One day early in the school year at this insane place some recent graduates who practiced Kenpo Karate came on campus and gave us a demonstration. I was absolutely hooked. Although I'd played some basketball and football, I immediately felt that Karate was my sport. I quickly signed up and began taking weekly lessons. The instructor's name was Oliver Lucas and he held the classes in a large second floor room in his house. I advanced very quickly and loved every minute of it. The main focus of Oliver's training was street fighting so we did a ton of sparring. After every lesson we would go home with bruises all over our arms and legs. I had been in fights at school but never really knew "how" to fight. Now I did, and I couldn't wait to try out my new found skills on the first person to mess with me.

All of the influences from karate were negative. There was not one Christian in the place. It seemed that everywhere I turned I just found people who would reinforce my hatred and anger. Karate did give me an opportunity to release some of this anger in a marginally controlled environment. I got to injure other people without getting into trouble.

I finally hit rock bottom the summer before high school. Emotionally I felt like "broken glass" on the inside. The hate I had for my dad began to transform into "self" hate. I hated my life. I began to think about suicide almost every day. Every night I went to bed with my Marine Corp knife trying to get up enough nerve to slit my wrists. Finally one night that summer I reached the end of what I could take. For those who struggle with depression and suicide you can reach a point where it is so incredibly painful just to be alive that you'll do anything to stop the pain. My best friend from 6th grade chose drugs to numb his pain. I chose a different option.

One evening as my family was watching television in the other room I calmly wrote my suicide note and placed it in a conspicuous place in my room. I went into the kitchen, found a bottle of aspirin and took as many as I could swallow. I then went back to my room and waited to die. In the morning I was still very much alive but had a terrible pain in my stomach. I had failed. I was determined to do a better job the next time. And that's when God stepped in.

At my next Karate lesson something unusual happened. Our instructor Oliver wasn't there. This had never happened before. Also, for the first time ever we had a visitor, a guy who studied Taekwondo Karate. This was the only time he visited our class. Toward the end of each class we always paired off to spar. Sparring is where you fight one-on-one against your opponent. Because I was not yet a brown belt I had not been trained to block head shots (punches or kicks to the head). These were not allowed in class or in tournaments until you had reached that belt level. As fate would have it I ended up getting paired up with the visitor.

We had only sparred for a few minutes when he threw a round house kick to the left side of my face. My

started a Christian Club at my high school. I hired a Christian band to perform during the lunch hour at my public school. I became a counselor at Christian camps. I began researching scientific creationism and would turn in papers at school arguing against evolution. I tried to present one of these in a class my freshman year. I got about three minutes into my presentation and my science teacher shut me down. All of the considerable energy I had channeled into anger and hatred just a few months earlier was now focused on telling others what an amazing thing God had done for me.

At home things were much better. The anger and hatred were gone. Interestingly enough God didn't change my dad. In fact he never changed, but with age became a little more tolerable to be around. God didn't change my circumstances but instead changed me, changed my perspective. I have met many Christians who grew up in the church and made a decision for Jesus very early in life. Then there are people like me who had to hit rock bottom before they would believe. Because of my experience, because of this contrast in my life, I am so incredibly grateful for what God did for me. God delivered me "from death to life".

THREE

A Prodigal Son

After I became a Christian I continued to attend the same "dead" church I mentioned earlier. Because of this I never grew much spiritually. The church's "cast" system was even more rigorous in high school so I slowly became disenchanted again with Christians. There was one "trigger" incident that pushed me over the edge. My dad's printing job allowed him to have summers off, allowing us to travel.   The summer between 10th and 11th grade I was gone from California for more than a month.   I remember thinking that when I showed up for Sunday school at least some of the kids would ask where I had been, or say "It's great to see you again". That wouldn't be the case.

I walked in with a friend from my public school who was much higher in the cast system.   When we walked in together they completely ignored me and immediately began engaging my friend.   It was like I didn't exist. That was it for me. I decided at that point to pursue acceptance at my public school, since I couldn't find any at church. I made the same mistake many new Christians do by focusing on "people" rather than on "Jesus".

During my senior year in high school I was elected to student government and had become very popular at school. I had lots of friends and most of them were not Christians. Sadly, these non-Christian friends showed me more kindness and acceptance than most of the kids at my church. It is interesting to me that when I decided to walk away from my faith; Satan had a group on non-believers ready to welcome me with open arms.

In college I moved into the dorms on campus and stopped attending church all together. Slowly I began to drift away from God. By the time I graduated from college I was completely backslidden. If you would have asked me at that point in my life if I was a Christian, my answer would have been "I used to be".

In college God put wonderful Christian students into my path but I ignored them. I worked as a Resident Advisor in the dorms. One of the other RAs in my dorm was a strong Christian guy and a cancer survivor. I often thought about talking to him about my backslidden condition but just blew it off. God kept trying, and I kept ignoring Him.

Unfortunately my experience was not unique. In 2011 the Barna Group concluded a five-year study comprised of eight national studies, which was done on teenagers and young adults between the ages of 18 to 29. It found that nearly three out of every five young Christians (59 percent) disconnect from church life, either permanently or for a long period of time after the age of 15. Those polled were active in a Christian church during their teen years.

I believe that one of the reasons that most young people are disconnecting from Christian churches is because so many churches are spiritually bankrupt. Cathy and I experienced this first hand during our two relocations. Prior to leaving Southern California we had attended Calvary Chapel in Diamond Bar California for almost 12 years.

Calvary Chapel is the only church I've found that takes the Bible's requirement seriously to "teach the whole counsel of God" Acts 20:27. So our pastor, like all other Calvary Chapel pastors, taught through the entire Bible, from Genesis to Revelation. This would typically take several years to complete. As a result, people who attend these churches, including young people, grow spiritually strong. They truly know the Bible from cover to cover.

When we looked for a new church first in Cincinnati and then in Dallas we were horrified by what we found. Nearly every Christian church we attended in both cities was doing anything but teaching God's word. Some were like watching an episode of Oprah. One pastor kept talking about the three little pigs and would play clips from R-rated movies like Silence of the Lambs to try and make some "spiritual" point!

At one church they played some new age type music while we watched a video of a man swimming under water in a tuxedo! At yet another church we attended the pastor and his wife sat together on the stage and talked about their "relationship"! Jesus and His Word were nowhere to be found.

Having spent more than a decade in a rock solid church like Calvary Chapel, we had no idea about the condition of the church in general. It is a complete mess. It is no wonder to me that most young people want nothing to do with church once they leave home. It's easy to leave something that has had no impact on your life.

The Bible anticipated and predicted that this would happen in the last days. In II Timothy 4:3 we read "For the time will come when they will not endure sound doctrine, but according to their own desires, because they have itching ears, they will heap up for themselves teachers; and they will turn their ears away from the truth, and be turned aside to fables."

This is "exactly" what has happened to the Christian church in America. If you are a parent and this describes your church, it is critical that you make the effort to find a church that teaches the Bible, chapter by chapter, verse by verse. While it's not a guarantee that you children's faith will endure, it will certainly improve their odds.

A second reason why I believe young people are leaving the Christian church is because they don't see

Christianity being lived out in the lives of their parents. So many parents "talk the talk" but don't live a life in obedience to God's Word. So when their children compare their parents to non-Christian parents they see no real difference. Or as in my case they see only Pharisees, people who are outwardly religious but who are dead spiritually.

It's difficult for me to write about this 10-year period when I walked away from my faith. Before I became a Christian I rarely felt convicted when I sinned. However, during this period in my life I never felt comfortable with how I was living. I had tasted life and was now returning to the filth that I had known previously. I can say that the one miracle during this 10 year period is that God prevented me from making a complete wreck of my life.

There is a verse in the Old Testament book of Joel where God says "I will restore to you the years that the locust have eaten." The locust had already consumed the first 14 years of my life and now they were consuming another 10. But God is His infinite kindness would eventually restore these lost years.

FOUR

Cathy

I finished college and started my first job where I met Cathy. We both attended the same university and earned the same Bachelor's degree in Business Administration. We went to a large California State University. Because I graduated three years before her, our paths never crossed in college. We both went to work for the same business services company after college. I took an entry level management position and she started out as a Client Service Representative. We dated for a few months then decided to get married. Cathy was raised in the Catholic Church and I had not attended church in years so I didn't give much thought to her spiritual condition.

A few years into our marriage we began thinking about starting a family. It was during this time that I felt the Holy Spirit calling me back into a close relationship with God. I had been fighting this conviction for years. There was a terrific church I had attended a couple of times called Calvary Chapel in West Covina, California. The church had just moved to a new location less than ten minutes from our home. Cathy and I began attending every Sunday morning.

This was the kind of church I wish I had found and attended right after I became a Christian. The people there were from all walks of life and from many different ethnic groups. In spite of the tremendous ethnic diversity in Southern California, the church I grew up in was 99% white. The teaching at Calvary Chapel was rock solid. After attending for several months I recommitted my life to Christ. I asked God to forgive me for the many sins I had committed in the previous 10 years. As He always does He welcomed me back with open arms.

I began to encourage my wife to consider a personal relationship with Jesus. That's when the fights started. We argued all the time. She was so attached to the rituals of her Catholic faith.

I remember one Sunday after church we sat in the parking lot of a grocery store arguing about Catholicism versus Christianity. She ended our conversation by saying that if we ever had children she didn't want them to attend Calvary Chapel. I felt strongly that our marriage was going to end. I became incredibly depressed but continued to pray for her salvation.

The very next Sunday we were sitting in church. As was always the case the pastor, Raul Ries, gave an invitation and asked those who did not have a relationship with Jesus to come forward and say a prayer. I was absolutely shocked when Cathy stood up and walked forward. I can still remember where we were sitting. I couldn't believe it. God had done the second significant miracle in my life by saving my wife and our marriage. That was January 1996 and one year later our first child, Lauren, was born. God prevented us from having children until we were both on the same page spiritually.

Cathy - I met Duane at work when he gave a presentation at my department's staff meeting one day. My first thought of him was, "I'd like to marry that guy!" We began dating by going out to lunch together. He had dated many girls in college and at work. I didn't think our dating would last long and that I'd be just another girl on his "list".

I was in love and desperately wanted our relationship to last so I "prayed". I'd never prayed before or asked anything specific from God. I remember every detail of that moment of my first prayer. I lay in bed with my feet up against the wall, during the middle of the day, hoping Duane would ask me out on a date again. I made a deal with God. If He would allow our relationship to continue, I would serve Him all my life. I didn't know what I was telling God. I was just a love-smitten young girl.

To my surprise and everyone else's, Duane suggested that we buy a house together while we were driving to dinner one evening. I told him I would not live with someone outside of marriage. He said,

"We'd be married, of course." I guess you could say that this was his version of a romantic marriage proposal. Duane proposed just three months after we began dating and we were married six months later.

Our first year of marriage was very difficult. Duane was not living out his faith or following the Lord and I wasn't yet a Christian. I grew up in a religious home attending Mass every Sunday. It was a ritual that I participated in but it lacked any meaning for me. I didn't know a single Bible story because I had never read the Bible. I was taught there was a God, that Jesus was the Son of God, that Jesus died for my sins and there's a Heaven and a Hell. They were just facts, something I knew in my head but meant nothing to my heart and soul. I believed in God, I just didn't believe He was my personal God. I prayed repetitive prayers that I'd heard a thousand times. I would recite them by rote memory. I couldn't imagine talking to God in a "personal" way and on a daily basis.

Our marriage had a rocky start because I was selfish and strong willed. I insisted on having my way. I thought marriage was about having someone who would make me happy. How wrong I was. My Godly mother-in-law heard of our marital trials and began earnestly praying for my salvation and our marriage.

We thought about having children. I adore kids and wanted children right away. Wanting to be responsible future parents, Duane and I decided we should agree on a church to attend before starting a family. Church shopping nearly led us to divorce. Ironic, isn't it?

We started attending different churches from various denominations but we finally settled on Calvary Chapel. Everything bothered me about this church. The worship music was too loud and concert-like. I was accustomed to solemn, angelic-like choir music. And it annoyed me immensely that people wore whatever they wanted to church. Weren't they supposed to be in their Sunday best instead of shorts and sandals?

Everything the Pastor quoted from the Bible disturbed me and contradicted my views about how to get to Heaven. I thought being a good person was the only requirement to getting into Heaven. There was an enormous amount of turmoil and struggle in my heart. I was angry that someone was telling me that my knowledge of God was incomplete and wrong.

Duane kept taking us to the same church, week after week, where I would hear the gospel and detailed teaching from the Bible. I became increasingly annoyed with what I was hearing and with Duane. We would have heated arguments in the car after church. I concluded that we would never agree on faith or what church our family would attend. I didn't see any alternative except divorce.

Finally, on another dreaded Sunday of attending church with Duane, I heard the gospel presented again and an altar call given. The Pastor, Raul Ries, asked people to come forward if they wanted to pray and ask God to be their Lord and Savior. My heart was pounding and I knew that the Holy Spirit wanted me to give in. It was time to surrender to Jesus and let Him be my Savior and Lord. I stood up, went forward, wept, and prayed to Jesus! That's when my real life began.

It amazes me that God pursued me all my life. The Bible says in Romans 5:8 "That God demonstrates His love toward us, in that while we were still sinners, Christ died for us." God miraculously "cured" me when I was a malnourished infant. He "rescued" me and my family from a war torn country and delivered us to America. He "provided" for my needs through the generosity and kindness of Christian believers. He "answered" my prayer for a Godly husband. Jesus had His hands upon me all my life. He was good even when I wasn't. He was right there beside me all along.

FIVE

The Glass House

In Ephesians chapter 2 we read "For by grace you have been saved through faith, and that not of yourselves; it is the gift of God, not of works, lest anyone should boast. For we are His workmanship, created in Christ Jesus for **good works**, which God prepared beforehand that we should walk in them." These three verses are fascinating to me. The most profound truth from them is that no one can enter into Heaven through their own efforts or their own "good works". It is only through faith in Jesus.

When someone offers you a "gift" you don't reach into your wallet, pull out $20 and say "Here you go. Thanks for the gift." You simply accept the gift. That's how salvation and entrance into Heaven works. Jesus did all the work for us so all we have to do is put our faith in Him, accept Him as our Savior. It's so simple.

But what I also find amazing about these three verses is that while we are not saved "by" our good works, once we say yes to Jesus He gives us good works to do. Good works are evidence that someone is truly saved. And God has prepared specific good works for each of us as Believers. And these works are not our gift back to God for saving us; they are **His gift to**

us. Ministry is a gift from God to us, not the other way around. So many Christians are confused by this. After they accept Christ they feel they need to somehow pay God back for saving them through their own efforts. Nothing could be further from the truth.

Now that Cathy and I were on the same page spiritually, we could begin to discover the works God had set aside for us to do. It didn't take long for us to find lots of great stuff to do. At our church in Southern California they had an alter call at the end of each of the three morning services. As many as several dozen people would come forward at the end of each service. Cathy began working as a New Believer Counselor. She would meet with these new Believers right after they made a decision for Jesus.

My works were focused on street evangelism. I joined a group of about 20 people at our church that would go out to various places and share the gospel. We went to Hollywood, to malls, to small villages in Mexico and to Indian Reservations in Arizona. A few months after I joined this group one of the leaders suggested we visit a local punk rocker hangout. It had a large open area where young people would hang out. It also had a building called the Glass House that was used for punk rock concerts. That's what attracted the kids.

The Glass House was located in a high crime area. In fact the city where it is located has one of the highest crime rates in Southern California. To put it bluntly it is not the kind of place you would want to spend your evenings, unless you were homeless or wanted to catch a punk rock concert. No other ministries or churches were doing an outreach to this place. Several of us went there on a Saturday afternoon to check it out. The place was deserted since it was mid-day. We stopped in front of The Glass House and prayed that if this was where God wanted us to go next that He would bless our efforts.

Several members of our evangelism team began meeting at our home every other Saturday night around 8:00pm. We would have a time of fellowship and prayer and then put together hot dogs, chips and drinks to take to the Glass House. Someone had heard that a lot of the kids who hung out there were homeless so we decided to feed them every time we went there.

Our initial reception by the "core" group of punkers was chilly to say the least. This core group had a leader named Richard. When he heard what we were doing and where we were from, he jumped up on a small concrete wall and began dropping f-bombs on all of us. He rambled on for probably 10 minutes about how corrupt the church was and how "religion" was the source of all evil in the world. It was going to be an uphill battle.

However, we soon discovered that this was indeed where God wanted us to spend our time and efforts. The Glass House was where God had assigned us to do good works. Some nights there would only be a handful of kids there and other nights there would be hundreds of them. On the bigger nights there would be other groups there like anarchists and rockabillies. On a couple of occasions several Neo Nazis showed up. Local gang members would drop by from time to time. It was quite the melting pot. There were often fights and on the busier nights there was a large police presence.

Our approach was always the same. We would show up around 9:00pm and hand out the food. We would then break into smaller teams of two or three and walk around and talk to the kids until about 1:00am. Most of the kids were between the ages of 14 and 25.

My approach would be to introduce myself to a small group of kids and ask if it would be okay if I asked them a few questions about God and about Heaven. I would ask them what they think happens to people when they die and what determines if someone makes it into Heaven. I would then ask them what they thought the Bible said about how to get into Heaven. Roughly 90% of the time their answers were not Biblically correct so I would then ask if I could tell them what the Bible actually said. They almost always agreed. There were some amazing times when after I finished talking to someone I realized that the words I had spoken were not my own. They came from the Holy Spirit.

Some of our conversations would last a few minutes and some for more than an hour. Many of these kids began to make decisions for Jesus. There were so many amazing miracles that happened there during our two years at the Glass House. One night there were several hundred kids there. We decided to do a skit right in the middle of the plaza area. The skit required us to fall to the ground on several occasions. The problem was the ground was covered by glass from dozens of broken beer bottles. Also, the crowd that night was really amped up.

There were lots of fights and lots of police. About half way through our skit several dozen drunken punk rockers began screaming profanities at us. Then they started threatening us physically during the skit. I remember thinking at one point that at any minute someone was going to break a beer bottle across the back of my head.

Just as we were about to get pummeled the police came in and pulled them all away from us. Since a riot was about to break out we couldn't finish our skit. But then something amazing happened. Immediately after the police pulled them back we somehow broke into small groups and every single one of us was engaged in intense conversations with these kids for more than an hour. God turned the entire situation around in a matter of seconds. It was amazing.

There was another night when we weren't making any progress. When we met for a huddle after about one hour into our evening everyone had the same story. No one would talk to us. It was like there was a complete wall up that night. So we wrapped our arms around each other and stood in a circle and prayed. We basically said "God we are outnumbered tonight by the enemy. Can you please send us some help? Can you break through for us?"

What happened next was a miracle. Later that night when we had our last huddle we discovered that right after that group prayer everyone had an open door and several kids got saved. I think we sometimes underestimate the importance and power of prayer.

One evening I was talking to a young couple in their early twenties. It had been cloudy that day and looked like it could start raining at any time. The young woman was very interested and asked a lot of questions. As I was wrapping up our conversation I asked her if she would like to say a prayer to accept Christ. She quickly agreed and we prayed together. Literally as she was saying "amen" the sky opened up and it poured down rain. Everyone scattered to their cars. God held back the rain just long enough for this young woman to pass from death to life.

One night I was paired up with a team member named Ryan, but we called him "Vanilla" because he had a really pale complexion. Most members of our evangelism group had nick-names. Mine was Duane-O-Mack. I generally focus on "grace" when I share the gospel, but Vanilla was all about the "law", a real fire and brimstone type of guy. The funny thing is that Vanilla was a really small guy.

So one night we were talking to a gang member who was sitting on a concrete wall that was about two feet high. Vanilla was laying into him hard with a message of condemnation and judgment. I could tell this guy was getting really irritated with Vanilla. I started looking for an opportunity to insert myself into the conversation when the guy leaned to one side. Under his right leg was a huge knife. I remember thinking that Vanilla was going to get a free ticket to Heaven that night! Thankfully Vanilla survived and he went on to become a full-time missionary in Colombia.

There were so many memorable encounters but I'll share just one more because there is an important principle related to it. One night I was approached by a young man who was probably around twenty years old. As often happened in this area he asked me for money. I immediately felt an evil presence from him. He wasn't demon possessed but I felt that he was involved in demonic activity. I told him I would give him ten dollars if he would give me ten minutes of his time. He agreed. I began to share the gospel with him as well as my personal testimony.

During our conversation he kept backing up. Each time he would back up I would step forward so I could continue our conversation. This kept happening throughout our conversation. It was very strange. I literally had to follow this guy all over the place to finish our conversation. He said nothing the whole time. He didn't ask one question. I thanked him for listening, gave him a ten dollar bill and he walked away. After he left I understood what had happened.

Whenever I witness to someone I always quote several Bible verses. I typically spread them out at intervals during the conversation. I realized that every time I had quoted a Bible verse he had moved backward! He didn't move back when I talked about my personal life, or when I talked "about" what the Bible said. He moved back when I "quoted" the Bible. The Word of God is so powerful that the demonic influences in his life were physically repelled by God's Word.

Whenever I train others on how to share their faith I will often use this real life example to bring home the importance of quoting the Bible to others when sharing the Gospel. The Bible says in Hebrews 4:12 "For the word of God is living and powerful, and sharper than any two-edged sword, piercing even to the division of soul and spirit, and of joints and marrow, and is **a** discerner of the thoughts and intents of the heart." While I had always known this "intellectually", on that night I experienced it personally, and it was fascinating.

My hope the entire two years we spent at the Glass House was that their punk rock leader, Richard, would eventually make a decision for Christ. After we had been going to the Glass House for about one year he actually began to look forward to our visits. He became a type of ambassador for us, introducing us to visiting punk rockers from other areas of Southern California.

I was sitting with Richard one evening having small talk when he told me he was going to give up hard liquor. Just for a second I got excited thinking a breakthrough was coming until he finished his thought. He said that hard liquor was irritating his stomach so he was switching back to marijuana! This was one of those situations that was sad and funny at the same time. Richard never accepted Christ during the two years we spent with him but I sure hope to see him one day in Heaven. I really liked him.

I share these details with you to demonstrate that as soon as I returned to my faith God had a list of "good works" waiting for me. And these works were a perfect fit for me. Do you recall how I started my life, full of rejection, anger and profanity. Well that's what these kids at the Glass House were all about. That was their story, so I could relate to them perfectly. They were like broken glass on the inside, just like me. God sent me to them because I understood them. God knew that I would love them even as they were spewing profanity at me. God knew that when I looked at them, I would see myself from 20 years earlier, and I would have tremendous compassion for them. And I did.

The sad thing for me is that from my late teens to my late twenties I walked away from God. During that 10 year period I missed out on countless good works that God had intended for me to accomplish. I can never get those opportunities, those good works back again. The same is true for you. God has a list of good works for you as well. If you are not yet a Christian, or you are a Believer but you have neglected your relationship with God, you are missing out on an incredible adventure. The Christian life is anything but boring, at least when you're doing the work God has called you to do!

SIX

Our First Home

When Cathy and I were still engaged we began looking for a home to purchase. I lived in an apartment and she still lived with her parents. We hadn't saved up enough for a down payment by the time we were married so after our wedding the two of us lived in her parent's house for a few months.

We had been keeping in touch with a local builder during Phase I and Phase II of their development in the Southern California city of Chino Hills. Three months after we were married we had saved enough to buy a home in Phase III. In each phase they built roughly 20 homes all at once. There was so much demand at that time for new homes in the entry level price range that the builder held a "lottery" session at the beginning of each phase. All interested, pre-approved buyers would show up on a Saturday and put their names into a basket. The Sales Representative would pull names out one at a time to determine who would get to pick the first lot, then the second lot, and so on.

Because we had kept in contact with the builder during the previous two phases they remembered us when we returned for Phase III. When we visited them in the Fall of 1992 the Sales Rep had some exciting news for us! Because their larger, more expensive homes (which we could not afford) were not selling well, they decided to build the smaller homes up on the hill, and on larger lots! (Many of the homes in Chino Hills have very small yards.) This meant that we would have a much bigger yard, since they were putting homes that were roughly 1,500 square feet on very large lots!

But then she said something that shocked us. She said that because we had stayed in contact with her, she would let us **skip** the lottery process and pick the first home site prior to the lottery! We couldn't believe it! That meant we would have the best lot in phase III! We were so excited that we immediately drove up the hill with a map she provided and found an absolutely amazing lot.

This lot stood head and shoulders above all the others. It was roughly one quarter of an acre, which was extremely large by Chino Hills' standards. It was right next to a hiking trail so there would be a large gap between us and the next house. It was on a hill that dropped off sharply behind the lot so there would be no homes behind us at all, just a nice view of the San Gabriel Mountains. It was perfect! I remember we both ran around the lot like teenagers high-fiving each other! We still went to the lottery meeting just to see who our new neighbors would be. Roughly four months later we moved into our beautiful new home and lived there for 12 years. Our first two children would start their lives in this home on Valley High Drive.

To this day it still makes no sense why the Sales Representative let us skip the lottery and pick the best lot. We didn't deserve this incredible gift and it certainly wasn't fair to the other buyers. Cathy was not yet a Christian and I was still a prodigal son. Why would God bless us in this way when we were not His children? The answer is that **God is good**. He is good to those who know Him and even to those who do not, because that is His nature. The Bible says in Romans 2:4 that it is God's kindness that leads us to repentance. Matthew 5:45 says that God makes the sun to rise on the evil and the good, and sends rain on the just and on the unjust.

I believe there was another reason. Because God knows all things He knew that Cathy would eventually say yes to Jesus, and that I would return to the faith I had walked away from in college. He knew that 10 years later this home would be a place where members of an evangelism team from our church would meet, worship and pray before going out to share the Gospel on Saturday nights with punk rockers and homeless kids. He knew that this house would one day be used to advance His kingdom. And so God stepped into our lives and performed a miracle.

SEVEN

The Parking Meter

Because my wife Cathy and I grew up in Southern California, we spent a lot of time at the beach. When Lauren was around six months old we were planning a day trip to Huntington Beach when we hit a snag. I don't remember why but for some reason it would have been much more convenient to go to the beach on Sunday than on Saturday. We considered skipping church and going on Sunday but didn't think that would be right. We reorganized our schedule and headed to Huntington Beach on Saturday.

For those reading this who are familiar with that area you know that parking can be a nightmare. There are lots of parking spaces along the beach but they are usually all taken unless you get there really early. For some reason there were dozens of empty parking spaces that Saturday. I randomly pulled into one and started pulling out the "mountains" of baby stuff we had brought with us. Once everything was out of the car and on the middle island I looked in our change drawer for a few quarters. We only planned on staying for a couple of hours so 8 quarters were all we needed. "No problem" I thought.

Well there was only "one" quarter in the change drawer, which was really unusual. Like most people we always kept lots of change in the car's ash tray. No problem I thought once again. Cathy always had lots of change in her purse. No luck. I couldn't believe it but she had "no" quarters. I looked under the seats in the car. Still no luck. I got a little irritated because we had a mountain of stuff on the curb and I didn't want to have to put it all back in the car. So there we were, the three of us, wondering what to do next.

I looked both ways on the street but couldn't see any businesses close by where I could get some quarters. Cathy was standing near the back of the car near Lauren and I was standing near the front, on the driver's side. I looked toward them and told Cathy to stay there with Lauren while I hiked down the road to try and get some change.

As my body moved to my left, toward them, it was as if something (or someone) grabbed my head and turned it to the right and toward the ground. It was probably a strange site, my body going one direction and my head turning the other way. I froze. I couldn't believe what I was seeing. There on the ground about an inch from my driver's side front tire was a stack of quarters! I turned to Cathy and, with a huge smile on my face, gestured toward the ground. She couldn't believe it either. I picked up the quarters to see how many were there. Seven! The exact number we were short!

I've often tried to calculate the odds of what happened that day. I love statistics so a little math will give you an idea of how big this miracle was. In order to calculate the odds for something like this you have to use compound probability. For example, if you flip a coin the odds of a "heads" coming up are of course 50%. However, if you flip that same coin a second time the odds of a "heads" coming up again are not 50%, they're 25%. You have to multiply .50 times .50. The odds of throwing three "heads" in a row with the same coin would be .125% (.50 x .50 x .50) and so on.

The first thing to consider is the probability of us going to the beach on the exact day when that little stack of quarters was waiting for us. I'll be generous here and say we would only have gone during the summer months, so those odds are 1 in 90, or .011. Next you need to consider the odds of my choosing the correct parking space, given that there were dozens of open spaces that day. I'll be conservative again here and say 1 in 50, or .02. It gets tougher when you try to estimate the probability of someone not only leaving a stack on quarters on the ground, but the exact number we needed. Even being extremely conservative again the odds could not be better than 1 in 1,000, or .001. We'll ignore some other factors and just do the math on these three.

If you multiply .011 x .02 x .001 you get 0.0000022 or one chance in 500,000. With a more complete list of factors I'm sure the true number is more like one in a million! The amazing thing to me is not that God did such an incredible miracle that Saturday morning; it's that He went out of His way for a need that was **so small**. It would not have been the end of the world for me to walk a quarter of a mile down the road to get some change. But because God cares about even the most trivial needs in our life, He does things like this. No detail is too small to escape His attention. There is another message in this. God didn't give us four or five quarters that day, He gave us seven, the exact number we needed. Sometimes God gives us more than we need, but never less than we need. That's His character.

For Cathy's next birthday after this little parking meter miracle I gave her a professionally made plaque with seven quarters glued to the front and the following Bible verse on the bottom: "And my God shall supply all your needs according to His riches and glory in Christ Jesus". Philippians 4:19. This plaque is still prominently displayed in our home office and is a constant reminder of God's provision and that He cares about even the seemingly insignificant needs in our lives.

EIGHT

Waiting on God

When our first child Lauren was born, Cathy tried going back to work but it only lasted a few months. We both agreed that she should be a stay-at-home mom. My wife is a wonderful, attentive mother so the stay-at-home mom role was a perfect fit for her. This change, however, meant almost a 40% decrease in our family income. My prospects for immediate advancement at worked looked dim at the time so I began looking for another company to work for. This would turn out to be a huge mistake.

At the time, I had been working for my company for almost ten years, ever since graduating from college. It was a great place to work. The company was very large and had many offices around the country. I was "lucky" enough to work in what many employees considered to be the best office. However, I felt that I needed to move to another company in order to increase my income. It wasn't long before I got a call from a company in Orange County offering me a significant increase in my base pay. Even though there were many warning signs I accepted their offer without much thought.

I ended up going to work for a company that I later discovered was listed in a business magazine as the

#1 worst company to work for in California! A good analogy for this job change would be leaving a job with Nordstrom and taking a position at a pawn shop. It was a horrible experience and I was devastated. I began praying like never before and within ten months I had a job back at my old company, just at a different location. I had a much longer commute to work, one hour versus 15 minutes, but the increase in my salary and bonus almost made up for the loss of Cathy's income.

In the end God worked a miracle and came to my rescue after I made a terrible mistake. But there's more to this story. Remember how I mentioned earlier that I felt I had no chance for an increase in my pay? Well about one year after I left my company my previous boss was fired. It turned out that at the time I left he was having an affair with a female manager I worked with. We both reported to him. She was married at the time and had two kids.

During the time they were having the affair he convinced HR to implement a huge increase in the pay grade for the position we both held. If I had stayed in my old job I would have benefited from this quid-pro-quo arrangement. I would have achieved the same base pay increase without going through that horrible experience of working for the worst company in California, and I would have maintained my 15 minute commute to work.

This story had a dramatic ending for my former co-worker and former boss. My co-worker's husband got suspicious and began following her after work. He quickly discovered her infidelity. He confronted her and attacked her physically one evening at their condo. In an attempt to save her life she jumped from the second story window of their condo. She broke an ankle but managed to escape. Her husband barricaded himself in their condo and a SWAT team had to be called out. He eventually surrendered to the police. Once the story broke it wasn't long before my former employer figured out what had happened and fired my former boss.

There is an obvious lesson here. I have learned the hard way that when I find myself in a difficult situation it is so incredibly important to **wait on God**. I should never try to "take matters into my own hands", but rather put matters in His hands, and then wait for direction. And I need to pray diligently about my situation and ensure I have a peace in my heart about what actions to take. In this situation, I didn't need to take any action at all. God had a **perfect** solution for me if only I had been patient and waited for Him to deliver it to me.

NINE

Ryan

Our son Ryan was born when our daughter Lauren was just over two years old. When we arrived at the hospital the ultrasound revealed that Ryan was turned the wrong direction so they told us Cathy would need a C-section. It was a bit of a shock and quite emotional for Cathy. We all headed to surgery and Ryan was delivered in good condition. As when Lauren was born I took two weeks off from work.

Due to the surgery Cathy needed my help moving around the hospital room. I had to partially hold her up on several occasions. Within an hour of arriving home from the hospital I began to feel a terrible pain in my lower back. Apparently I had strained the muscles in my lower back while helping Cathy in the hospital. Suddenly the pain because so intense that I literally couldn't move. I found myself lying on our couch in agony.

Cathy could hardly move due to her surgery. So we had a newborn baby and a two year old, and Cathy and I could barely move. It was a mess. I called my neighbors from across the street. They are a wonderful Christian family with kids about the same age as ours. They took Lauren from us and picked up a prescription for me at the local pharmacy. Within a few hours I was almost back to normal.

The next two weeks were fairly routine. Cathy was nursing Ryan just like she had Lauren. He seemed happy and healthy. Then on Friday afternoon of the second week while I was rocking Ryan he suddenly threw up. Every parent knows the difference between a baby spitting up and throwing up. I was a little bit concerned. Then he threw up several more times. This should not have happened since he was nursing. We called our pediatrician and she told us to take him to the ER immediately.

By the time we arrived at the hospital we were starting to get really scared. Ryan was less than two weeks old. The ER ran some blood tests and we waited for the results. After what seemed like an eternity they told us that Ryan had a very serious infection and that they had to take him by ambulance to a pediatric ICU facility. We were in shock. He was completely healthy just a few hours earlier. We were not allowed to ride in the ambulance so we drove to the ICU. When they finally let us see him it was horrible. He was in a see-through ICU box with all kinds of tubes going into him. He was looking at us and screaming but we couldn't pick him up. As I looked at him I remember feeling like someone was reaching into my chest and pulling out my heart. I felt an indescribable pain.

The only thing we could do for Ryan was pray. Cathy was part of a women's Bible study group that had a formal prayer chain system in place. Cathy called a couple of the women who in turn called others, asking them all to pray. That was the only women's Bible study Cathy ever attended that had a formal prayer chain, which I find interesting given the timing of Ryan's illness. We called every Christian family member and friend we could think of and asked them to pray for Ryan's healing. My guess is that we had more than 100 people praying for Ryan that night.

The ICU would not allow us to spend the night at their facility so we went home that Friday evening. Needless to say we didn't sleep much that night. We arrived back at the ICU the next morning right as they opened for visitors. When we asked for an update on Ryan we were amazed by the response. They told us that the blood work they did for him that morning showed no infection. They said that the hospital ER must have made a mistake when they did their testing, because it wasn't possible to go from his level of infection to no infection in one night. We of course knew differently. We knew he was very sick and that God had healed him in one night. We took him home that Saturday afternoon and I went back to work on Monday as originally planned.

This episode with Ryan had a profound effect on me. I had been somewhat casual about having a second child. Not that it wasn't special, it just felt routine. I sort of took him for granted before he got sick. That all changed after he spent that night in the ICU. I began to cherish my time with him and appreciate him, and these feelings haven't diminished over the years.

Cathy - We were blessed to have Ryan born on Good Friday. I recall being in the hospital celebrating our newborn baby boy on Easter Sunday! Even though I was in a lot of pain from having an emergency C-section, the joy of holding Ryan's hands in mine was well worth it.

When Ryan suddenly became ill with an infection and had to be in an incubator, it broke my heart to see him in the glass box with numerous tubes attached to him. I felt so helpless and knew only God could heal him. I contacted friends in my Bible study group and asked them to activate the prayer chain. It involved one mom calling another mom and praying together over the phone. The mom receiving the phone call then contacted another mom and the two of them would pray together. It was "prayer tag"!

The process would continue until every woman in the Bible study group had been contacted. That meant there were hundreds of prayers being lifted up for Ryan and it gave me great hope and comfort during one of the worst days of my life.

When Duane and I returned to the hospital the next morning to visit Ryan, the doctors and nurses said Ryan was fine. He had no sign of infection. His infection mysteriously cleared up overnight during the prayer tag. We knew it wasn't a mystery but a miracle. God had healed our little boy.

TEN

LAX

When Lauren and Ryan were young I was traveling for work between Southern California and the East Coast. The three hour time difference made these trips exhausting. Meetings often started at 8:30am but my body felt like it was 5:30am. On one of these trips I had a full day of meetings back east and then flew home that night. By the time I landed at Los Angeles International Airport (LAX) it was around midnight and I was completely exhausted. I have never been able to sleep on airplanes.

Because it was a short 3-day trip I had parked at the airport rather than at long term parking. As I walked to my car I began dreading the one hour drive home that was ahead of me. As I pulled out of my parking space and started to wind down through the parking structure I immediately found myself stuck behind a car that could not have been going more than file miles per hour! I couldn't believe it! It was the middle of the night and here was this insane person going so slow that I could have passed them in a wheel chair!

I thought that maybe they were just looking for an open space but quickly realized they were exiting, since they passed by several empty parking spots without pulling in. By the time I had followed them through a couple of levels within the parking structure I thought I was going to lose my mind!

I have traveled for work for more than 20 years and have never experienced anything like this. It was impossible to pass this car because of how narrow the parking garage was. I was stuck. Just as I began to have a complete emotional meltdown I suddenly felt an unexpected calm come over me. My blood pressure dropped back down to normal and I just accepted the fact that there was nothing I could do about my situation.

For what seemed like an eternity I followed this car then exited the airport. It had started raining just as I landed at LAX, which meant an even "longer" drive home. Just as I exited the airport and entered the freeway onramp I saw it. An accident had occurred just minutes before on the curved onramp. I remember staring into the face of a female driver whose car was turned the wrong direction on the freeway onramp. She looked like she was in shock. Then it occurred to me. God had just saved me from being part of this accident.

I am by nature not a patient person. I become frustrated when things don't happen on my schedule. And most of the time God's schedule is very different than mine. I want something right now but God says "wait" or even worse, He is silent. I'm not good at waiting. The Bible says over and over again to "wait on the Lord". There are so many examples in the Bible of people who refused to wait on the Lord and paid a huge price. King Saul refused to wait for Samuel to arrive to bless a feast. For this and other sins of disobedience God eventually took the kingdom from Saul and gave it to David.

You might be stuck in a difficult marriage, or report to an unfair boss at work, or have a child who is rebelling. Rather than take matters into your own hands, put your situation into the hands of the One who loves you with a perfect love. Wait on the Lord. He won't let you down.

ELEVEN

America's Most Wanted

In 2001, I had an opening for a Client Service Representative. One of the resumes I received caught my attention because the candidate had worked for several of our clients and claimed to have excellent knowledge of our company's software. It can be a huge win to find a strong candidate who is a former customer. They require minimal training and can truly empathize with clients, having been a client themselves. The one unusual thing was that she lived in Chicago but was applying for my position in Southern California. It was rare for me to fly someone to our office for an interview. However, she really impressed me during her phone interview so I had HR arrange for her to travel to my office for an interview.

She was very professional and had an excellent working knowledge of our software. I had another Manager, Greg, and HR interview her and they were equally impressed with her qualifications. The candidate was willing to pay for her relocation to California. I finished interviewing the other candidates and decided that this woman from Chicago was my best choice. Everyone else agreed so I asked HR to begin working on an offer letter, which would take a couple of days. Once I had the offer letter I was going to call her and formally offer her the position.

The day after I asked HR to get started on the offer letter, Greg just happened to be taking a technical training class in our Branch. Several employees from our Chicago office had flown in to take the same class. In our Division, classes were not always available in local branches so we would occasionally travel for training.

During one of the breaks in their class the employees from our Chicago office told Greg about a situation that had happened recently in Chicago. A woman had been taking jobs in HR or Benefits with various clients and then stealing the identities of her co-workers. Her HR positions gave her access to everything she needed to practice identity theft. At each company, she obtained credit cards in the names of her coworkers and ran up thousands of dollars in fraudulent charges. Before they could catch her she would disappear only to resurface later at another client and repeat the exercise.

Greg asked our Chicago employees what her name was. When they told him her name, Greg almost fell over and he literally ran downstairs to my desk. The woman I was about to hire was the same one stealing identities from client employees! I couldn't believe it!

We both went to HR and explained the situation. My HR Director told me that if she called me, to tell her that we had not yet made a decision on the position.

She then called Corporate HR for guidance. I took a closer look at the woman's resume and noticed something I'd missed. I knew she had worked for several of our clients but I hadn't noticed that she had worked in three different states in the Midwest. It was clear now from her resume that she was moving around from state to state to stay ahead of the authorities. She must have decided that it was too risky to stay in Illinois. California probably looked like a good place to start over far from the scene of her crimes.

This type of multi-state crime would have fallen under the jurisdiction of the FBI. My first thought was to call the FBI and give them her address and phone number, or better yet offer her the job then have them arrest her on her first day of work. But HR would not let me get involved. Corporate basically said that when she called back for a status to tell her that the requisition was cancelled due to budget constraints. When she called, that's exactly what I told her but I wanted so badly to say "I know who you are and what you're doing!" but I held my tongue.

After it was over I started thinking about how close I came to hiring one of America's Most Wanted. In her prior roles working for individual companies she probably had access to a few hundred employee records. Had she worked in our office she would have had access to well over one million individual employee records for more than 200 very large companies. I can't even imagine the damage she could have done to our company's reputation, not to mention the financial damage. What impact would this have had on my career? And I came within 24 hours of hiring her.

I also began to consider that incredible odds of these employees from our Chicago office being in our branch for this 2-day training class just as all this was occurring. And the only Manager from our office who attended the training was one of only three employees in our office who had interviewed her. And our Chicago employees just "happened" to mention what she had been up to in their city. The odds of this all coming together at exactly the right moment are so remote, I'm not sure they could be measured accurately. God stepped in and performed yet another unique miracle, and by doing so protected my company and me personally. And since God is a just God I'm sure she was eventually caught!

TWELVE

Maui

In the summer of 2001 my office qualified for what they call "Club". It is basically a long, 5-day weekend at a nice resort. Each qualifying office sends their GM and one member of their senior staff. That summer I was the newest member of the senior staff so in theory I had no chance of attending. To my amazement all six of my peers had other commitments that weekend or just didn't want to go to Maui. After everyone else said "no" my boss offered me the trip. Of course I said yes. Cathy and I got a free weekend in Maui. Everything was covered, even activities. My sister Donna stayed with our two children so we could go.

We had been to Maui twice already, once for our honeymoon and once with Lauren and Ryan, so we were familiar with the island. Cathy flew home one day early since my sister couldn't stay the entire time. Although being offered the trip was an amazing thing in and of itself, it was on my flight home that the real miracle occurred.

As I was sitting in my seat just before take-off I noted the empty seat next to me. I would learn later that it was the only empty seat on the plane. Given the long flight from Maui to LA I should have been thrilled to have the extra space, but instead I felt compelled to say a <u>very</u> brief prayer that went something like this: "God, if you will put someone in this seat who is searching for You I'll talk to them about You." That was it. It was one of the most casual prayers I've ever said. It was almost an afterthought.

Well just as the flight attendant started to shut the cabin door she hesitated. Suddenly a young woman came running onto the plane. She took the only available seat, the one right next to me. As soon as she was on the airplane they closed the cabin doors. Of course now I was on the hook. I had to keep my promise.

I was naturally curious why she had jumped onto our flight at the last minute so I asked her what had happened. She said she had been on standby all day for several flights but had no luck. She was working on a film in Maui and was trying to get home to LA to visit her family. She had decided to try one last time and if she couldn't get on this flight (my flight) she was going to give up and stay in Maui.

I asked her about the film she was working on in Maui. It was a Christian film. Well what a surprise. After a few more questions I basically knew her story. She was not a Christian. She was majoring in film at a college in Southern California and was working on this film as part of her degree program. What a "perfect" opening. She was very open to what followed next, which was me telling her my story and also telling her what the Bible says about salvation. We had a great conversation.

There is an unseen spiritual battle that occurs every minute for the souls of the lost. I have seen glimpses of this battle from time to time. In her case I would have loved to see the battle that occurred that day to get her the last seat on the plane, on my flight, and right next to me. I'd love to know how God prevented the person who bought the seat next to me from getting on the plane.

And I'm sure that all this occurred for one of two reasons: Either this young woman had a friend or relative praying for her salvation or her work on this Christian film caused her to want to know more about God. Either way, God put her next to me for five hours.

There is one prayer that God will answer "yes" 100% of the time. It is a prayer like the one I prayed. If you ask God to put people in your life who are open to or seeking the truth, God will always answer this prayer in the affirmative. In my case He answered it in less than five minutes! I hope to one day meet this young woman in Heaven. The Bible says that "one sows, another waters, but it is God who brings the increase." On that day God let me do a little "watering". It is the Holy Spirit who convicts unbelievers of their sin. Our job is to point them to Jesus and let God do the rest.

THIRTEEN

An Angel?

My second year in college I needed to satisfy a few elective classes. Foreign languages were one option. Since I had studied Spanish for two years in high school I looked into other languages that were being offered. For some reason Russian caught my attention. I borrowed the textbook that would be used for the class and showed it to my mom. Her response was that it looked too difficult and she discouraged me from taking the class. That sealed it for me. Whenever someone suggests I can't do something my reaction is to always prove them wrong, so I enrolled in the class.

Our professor was an elderly man named Dr. Zrimc. He had graduated from Harvard, taught seven different languages all over the world, had a photographic memory, and had survived a Nazi concentration camp in his home country of Yugoslavia. He was an absolutely amazing man so I knew I had made the right choice.

Dr. Zrimc was a brutal teacher who pushed us relentlessly and never missed an opportunity to insult and degrade us publicly if we did poorly on a test or quiz. In fact, on the very first day of class he got right up into a young girl's face and started asking her very roughly why she wanted to learn Russian. She burst into tears and ran out of the classroom. We never saw her again. Dr. Zrimc responded casually by saying "Well, that's one less student for me to worry about." We all hated him but we sure learned Russian.

My university was on the trimester system. In our first trimester of this class we had around 30 students. By the second trimester we were down to around 15. By the third and final trimester only five of us returned. The university was going to cancel the class due to low enrollment but we convinced them to let us finish off the year. We met in a small conference room for the third trimester.

In addition to studying the Russian language I also took classes in Russian geography, history and literature, again just for fun. As I began interviewing for jobs during my senior year I thought the CIA might find my interest in Russia appealing. I interviewed with them but was not offered a position. This was a good thing since a few years after I graduated, the Soviet Union collapsed and the Cold War ended. As a result the CIA engaged in some downsizing so this would very likely have been a very brief career path for me.

After I graduated from college and began my career, I continued my study of the Russian language at UCLA and through a private tutor. Eventually my career began to take off and I didn't have time to continue with this little hobby of mine. Then roughly 10 years later in 1999 I decided to take my first short-term mission trip to, of all places, Russia. This gave me a chance to finally practice my Russian, but I had forgotten a lot of what I had learned. However, the locals in Moscow kept telling me that the Russian I did speak while there was perfect. I had absolutely no accent. I sounded like a "local". This is a gift that God has given me, the ability to learn foreign languages quickly and to speak them without an accent.

When I returned from my short-term mission trip to Russia I couldn't shake the feeling that there was some small chance that I was supposed to do something more in Russia, but I didn't know what. On my drive back to Los Angeles after visiting a client in Santa Barbara, I stopped by a restaurant to grab some lunch. I was by myself so I sat in the bar area. That whole day I kept thinking about Russia. I had what I thought were "crazy" questions in my mind. Was I supposed to move our family there and become a full-time missionary? These thoughts seemed absolutely insane to me.

So this was my frame of mind as I sat there getting ready to order my lunch. As I stared at my menu, a man to my right whom I hadn't noticed interrupted my thoughts about Russia by asking me what I was having for lunch. He was standing at the bar area just to my right, not sitting down. He was sort of leaning against the bar. He was dressed very professionally and looked like someone that might be in Sales.

I told him I was going to have a turkey club sandwich. I looked down again at my menu for a few seconds then looked up again and he was gone. He never returned. But I noticed that behind him there was an elderly man and a young girl speaking a foreign language. I listened carefully and quickly realized that they were speaking Russian.

I was deep in thought concerning "what to do about Russia" and would not have noticed them if this mystery man had not interrupted me by asking what I having for lunch. So now I was even more stressed out. Was God telling me to take some small step, to see if I was supposed to do something more significant in Russia? And was this mystery man an angel sent to nudge me forward? I don't know. But the idea was just too crazy for me. After all, I had a good paying job with a great company, and we had a wonderful home in a terrific community. How could I possible consider walking away from all of that?

FOURTEEN

411

In 1999, a couple of years after returning to my company I was promoted to a Director position. In addition to a large pay increase I was moved from a cubicle to an office, which was really nice. I had a great group of mostly technical employees on my team. One downside to this promotion was I had to report to the GM, and he was very difficult to work for. The worst part was that he "claimed" to be a Christian, all the while using profanity and taking all of us out for drinks. Here I was reporting to another Pharisee, someone who was outwardly "religious" but completely "lost". He knew that I was a Christian and that my life was very different from his. I could tell he was uncomfortable around me.

In the summer of 2001, roughly 18 months after this promotion a friend from my old office told me about a Branch Manager opening in Phoenix. He said they were having difficulty finding someone for the job. This position would be a huge step forward for me in my career, as I would be running both the Phoenix and Denver offices. My only hesitation in applying was the knowledge of how badly my GM boss had treated others who had left our office to take other positions in the company. He had a reputation for retaliating against employees. I knew there could be risks if I applied.

I didn't have a peace about pursuing the job in Phoenix and financially we didn't need more money. I was already making enough to support our family. Also, my company had recently gone through two rounds of company-wide layoffs. Thousands of employees had lost their jobs. I should have waited on God for his direction.

I applied for the position in July of 2001 and interviewed in late August. They were still talking to other candidates on September 11, 2001. After 911 the national economy contracted and sales in our business unit disappeared. The Branch Manager position could no longer be funded. In fact the hiring Manager told me he had to come up with $800K in labor reductions. I wasn't getting the job.

A few weeks later our GM (my boss) let all of us who were part of his senior team know that there would be a third layoff sometime after January.   For the previous two rounds of layoffs he had told all of us at the same time during a staff meeting. This time he told me individually and then didn't give me additional details as he had in the past. It became obvious that he was hiding something.

In the subsequent months he became openly hostile toward me, criticizing me for any minor infraction. I began to think that he was going to put my name on his layoff list. I tried not to think about it. I honestly couldn't imagine someone who "claimed" to be a Christian retaliating against an employee for simply trying to advance their career. I was wrong.

On Thursday afternoon, April 11th 2002, he dropped by my office and asked me to come up to his office. He said he wanted to talk about Fiscal Year 2003. He didn't waste any time. He let me know that I would be included in the next round of layoffs. He handed me a severance package that included six months of salary continuation. Even though I had feared he would retaliate against me I never let myself believe it.

I asked him why I was included in the layoff and his exact words were "Sometimes I don't know why I do the things I do." As I was leaving he promised to help me find another job with the company. In fact he did just the opposite. In the subsequent months every time I applied for a position he told the hiring manager not to hire me. All of this from a man who taught Sunday school at his church!

I can barely remember the drive home. It was all a blur. There I was unemployed, with two preschool aged children and my wife Cathy a stay-at-home mom. I had been employed in some way or another since I was 15 years old. I worked several jobs in college to pay for school. For the first time in my life since my teenage years I didn't have a job. It was absolutely devastating.

I couldn't escape the stress of what had happened to me, not even in my dreams. I began having nightmares. In one dream I was laid off, called back to work, and then laid off a second time after only one month. In another dream I was in a senior staff meeting and my peers were all ridiculing me. During one of these nightmares I suddenly heard my mother's voice say my name and I immediately woke up. My mom had died three years earlier. From the way she called my name I could tell she was telling me to stop beating myself up over what had happened.

I don't know if God actually allowed my mom to call out to me, or if it was the Holy Spirit. But I do know that the voice I heard was absolutely that of my mom. After that day I never had another nightmare about my layoff.

I began looking for work month after painful month. The clock was ticking as I had only six months of salary continuation. The spring and early summer passed without a single phone call or job interview. I remember talking to God and saying "It has been 30 days so can this be over now". Then again at 60 days, and 90 days, and 120 days.

Then something interesting happened. The very week my two children went back to school my phone started ringing. It was as if someone turned on a faucet. I think God was saying, "Well you've had your five month paid vacation and since the kids are back in school it's time for you to go back to work." Within just a few weeks I was back to work, just two weeks before my unemployment insurance and salary continuation ran out!

God had delivered me again but not before giving me the longest paid vacation of my life. That summer I was able to take the kids to many fun places, including Sea World. We also took a family vacation to Yellowstone National Park in Wyoming. I also went on my second mission trip to Russia and had a wonderful experience. I remember my daughter Lauren, who was five years old at the time, saying how awesome it was to "have daddy home every day."

The Bible has much to say about people like my "religious" boss. In Matthew Chapter 7 beginning in verse 21 we read; "Not everyone who says to Me, 'Lord, Lord,' shall enter the kingdom of heaven, but he who does the will of My Father in heaven. Many will say to Me in that day, 'Lord, Lord, have we not prophesied in Your name, cast out demons in Your name, and done many wonders in Your name? And then I will declare to them, 'I never knew you, depart from Me, you who practice lawlessness!"

The Bible also says that in the Last Days people will have a "form" of Godliness but will not truly be Born Again. They will attend church, give to the poor and, yes, even teach Sunday school, and still end up lost eternally.

In Second Corinthians 13:5 the Apostle Paul says to "Examine yourselves as to whether you are in the faith." The obvious implication is that there are people who are convinced in their mind that they are going to Heaven even though they are completely lost. They are "religious" but don't have a "relationship" with Jesus. There is no fruit of the Spirit in their lives (love, joy, peace, patience, goodness, gentleness, self-control).

Some people will read this and say that only God knows who is going to make it into Heaven, and that is 100% correct. However, the Bible says we can know if someone belongs to Jesus by the fruit in their lives. If they don't have love for others, that's a pretty strong indication that they are not truly saved.

Over the years I have met dozens of religious people like my dad and my former boss. I've met them in my family, in church, in small group Bible studies, in my neighborhood and at work. Based on my personal experience these are by far the most difficult people to reach for Christ because they truly believe they are saved. I think this is why Jesus said to the religious leaders of His day that "Tax Collectors and sinners

will enter into the Kingdom of God before you will."
However, with God all things are possible. So if you
have a Pharisee in your life, keep praying!

I mentioned earlier that I hesitated for more than a
year before I started writing this book, and this
chapter is one of the reasons. I should have learned
my lesson from years earlier about waiting on God. I
pushed forward and pursued the Branch Manager job
in Phoenix even though I didn't have peace about my
decision. I am my own worst critic and even now a
decade later I still occasionally beat myself up over
this foolish mistake. Every April 11th I remember that
day, 411. I only hope that Lauren, Ryan and Hannah
will learn from my mistakes, wait on the Lord and
avoid the same agony.

FIFTEEN

A Job Miracle

After my layoff I went to work for a medical software company, managing their client service organization. This was my first and only experience working in the medical industry. The work environment was extremely unprofessional with employees and managers using foul language and harassing each other. Just before I arrived two female employees got into an argument. One slapped the other across the face. The one who was slapped chased the other employee through the building and tackled her! Both were still working there when I arrived, which gives you a sense of the culture.

I would sit in senior leadership meetings and watch VPs scream at each other, bang their fists on the conference room table and shout "We're not communicating! We're not communicating!" Since I had already worked for the worst company in California, I figured this one was probably second on that list! There were some positive times there. One of my employees told me she was a Christian and that she had been praying for several years that God would bring a Christian leader into the company.

I discovered how stressful this industry could be. One hospital said that a nurse was confused by our software and accidently gave insulin to a man who was allergic to insulin. He went into a coma and wasn't expected to live. They told us that they were going to sue us. Another hospital found a bug in our application that calculated doses for children's medicines. The labels were printing with exactly ½ the dose each patient should have received. Luckily a pharm tech noticed the error and called us before anyone was harmed. I couldn't believe that this company had not yet been sued out of existence.

The company made a huge strategic mistake just a couple of years before I joined them. Rather than focus on expanding their product within the United States, they got the bright idea to expand internationally. They sold and installed the product in Saudi Arabia, Japan, Canada and the UK. It was a huge disaster. Not only were the implementations a complete disaster, the effort drained scarce resources away from client support in the US. By the time I arrived in 2003 this company was on life support.

I made every effort to improve the professionalism of the client services department. I made some headway but the company overall continued to struggle financially. I was very happy to be employed again but working there really wore me out. Roughly ten months after I started working there I received a call from a woman named Lynn who worked for another large business services company. I had interviewed with Lynn when I was unemployed and she had seemed interested in me, but she didn't have an opening at the time. Interestingly enough I had applied for a Branch Manager position with her company, the exact job I had pursued at my old company that resulted in my layoff.

Lynn said that she now had an opening for a Branch Manager in Training position in Orange County. If I was hired for the job I would be in training for roughly one year and would then relocate to another part of the country and run my own office. It was a terrific opportunity. I talked it over with Cathy and we agreed that I should pursue the position. Unlike in the past, I prayed about this opportunity and had complete peace about taking the job. I interviewed with one of Lynn's peers in Sacramento and was offered the position.

A couple of days before I was going to give my two weeks' notice, rumors began to circulate through the office that our company was going to be bought by a much larger medical software company. If the rumors were true then many of our employees would lose their jobs. Everyone in the office was completely stressed out, except for me! I was walking around with this huge smile on my face. People would stop me in the hall and say "Why are you smiling? Haven't you heard the rumors?" Once again God had come to my rescue at **just the right time!**

On the very day I had planned on officially resigning they gathered us together for a big announcement. Our company was being bought out and there would be layoffs. The rumors were true. Later that day I gave my two weeks' notice. To my surprise the new owners offered me a "blank check" to stay. They had heard about the improvements I had made in client services and were willing to pay me nearly any amount to keep me.

I politely declined their offer but did give them a two hour debrief on all of the areas they needed to focus on to turn this business unit around. They were horrified by my description of the work environment but grateful for the information I provided. I can still remember the shocked looks on their faces as I described the horrors I had seen there in the previous ten months.

I ended up taking a wonderful vacation between jobs, renting a motorhome from one of my employees and camping at Lake Shasta in Northern California. Because this vacation was planned literally at the last minute there was only one campsite left when I called the campground. It turned out to be one of the best in the whole campground. Also, the family who camped next to us had a boat and offered to take all of us out on the lake. They were one of the friendliest families we had ever met.

As we enjoyed our vacation I couldn't help but note the amazing contrast. Here I was having an incredible time on beautiful Lake Shasta while this medical software company descended into chaos. I was about to begin a career with a company I had always admired, and a position that I thought was beyond my reach.

Think with me for a minute about all of the critical events that had to happen at just the right time for this to work out the way it did. What are the odds of the acquisition being announced the very day I had planned to resign? It's absolutely amazing.

SIXTEEN

Another House Miracle

After ten months in training, a Branch Manager position for the Cincinnati office became available. I couldn't even spell Cincinnati at the time! I had lived in Southern California my entire life so this was going to be quite the adventure for the four of us. My boss Lynn felt the Cincinnati job was a great opportunity. It was the worst performing office in the country, ranked 89 out of 89! Nowhere to go but up I reasoned.

God was about to perform a second miracle related to this job change. We had decided that Lauren and Ryan would attend Christian schools. Our city had decent public schools but we wanted our kids exposed to the Bible not just at home and at church, but at school as well. This was always a struggle however based on my income. But God had been faithful and Lauren had attended both a Christian preschool and Christian elementary school in our city, and Ryan a Christian preschool. We intended to continue this strategy in Cincinnati.

Our house sold in just a couple of weeks. We had bought our home in 1992 when prices were still depressed. When we sold it in the summer of 2004 it was near the "top" of the nationwide bubble in the housing market. Because of the timing, we made a tax free profit of $280,000! We had never imagined having that much money all at one time. It was yet another miracle. If we had sold just a few years earlier or later we would have missed this huge run-up in prices! If you have ever seen a chart on the housing bubble, especially for the California market, you'll know exactly what I mean. The year 2004 was a great year to sell.

Once we arrived in Cincinnati we found an amazing school called Cincinnati Hills Christian Academy. It was ranked as one of the top Christian Academies in the country! But like many great private schools it was expensive. We never could have afforded to send Lauren and Ryan there on my salary. That's why God allowed us to have such a large gain on our house. He honored our commitment to a strong Christian education for our children, and the money from the sale of our California home completely paid for a large portion of our home in Cincinnati and their school tuition for many years.

When I think of how my boss eliminated my job in retaliation for my applying for a job in another part of my company, I am reminded of the story of Joseph in the Old Testament. When Joseph's brothers sold him into slavery to Egypt, they meant it for evil, but God meant it for good. When my boss retaliated against me he also meant it for evil, but God meant it for good.

There were no K-12 Christian Academies in the area where we lived in Southern California. There were several Christian schools but most were not strong academically or spiritually. God wanted the **best** for our children and He accomplished this in a way that, to be honest, I would never have imagined or chosen.

Looking back now it all makes sense, but at the time it made absolutely no sense whatsoever. Quite honestly, if I had a choice I would have accomplished this some other way, some less painful way. But God was **testing** us, strengthening our faith, making us more mature. And giving us a **testimony** so that we could encourage other Believers who would go through a similar trial.

In his amazing book "A Future and a Hope", Pastor and Christian Author Jon Courson provides the following analogy of the benefits of going through these "trials" as Christians: A five-dollar iron bar can be pounded into a couple of ten-dollar horseshoes. Or, that same iron bar can be pounded further into $350 worth of needles. Or, that same iron bar can be pounded even further to produce $250,000 worth of fine watch springs. It all depends on how much pounding is done.

So if God is allowing you to be "pounded" right not, trust Him. He has a plan and a purpose, and He will deliver you.

SEVENTEEN

Another Job Miracle

Leaving all of our many friends, family members and our church and moving to Cincinnati was very emotional. We arrived in Cincinnati in early August just before school started. Our welcome in Cincinnati could only be described as a miracle. God knew how sad we were to be so far from "home" without friends or family members. What God did next was amazing. It was like he "backed up a truck" and gave us a mountain of wonderful friends through our kid's school, Cincinnati Hills Christian Academy (CHCA), my work and our wonderful neighborhood.

To our amazement, a CHCA parent who had only known us for a few weeks asked us what we were doing for Thanksgiving. We were still living in an apartment at the time. We said that we didn't have any plans. We weren't going to fly back home to California. She immediately invited us to join her family at their home for Thanksgiving! We were floored! This kind of thing doesn't happen in California, at least not to us!

This was a pattern that would repeat itself again and again in the coming months. God knew how sad we were, he knew we needed friends so he gave us a boatload. Ephesians 3:20 says that God is able to do exceedingly abundantly above all that we can think or ask. He certainly proved that to us in our move to Ohio!

God not only blessed us with great friends, but he blessed me with Chuck, one of the best bosses I've ever had. Taking on the worst performing office in the country was a huge, exhausting challenge. God knew I would need an extremely patient, supportive boss, so he gave me Chuck. God also did another miracle at work. Of the 80+ employees in my office there were only three rock solid Christians and one was named Vida. She went by "Vi" and her desk was the closest one to my office. This was yet another "coincidence". Vi was part of my accounting team but she also acted as my Administrative Assistant. But her most important role was providing me with much needed encouragement.

I faced some strong opposition in my efforts to turn that office around. Vi never missed an opportunity to quote Scripture to me and to lift my spirits! It is so amazing how God works in the lives of His children. He knows exactly what we need and when we need it. When he allows us to enter into trials He sends us wonderful believers like Vi to encourage us to keep going. And I needed a lot of encouragement.

Although I absolutely loved running my own office, fixing this severely underperforming branch was a huge challenge. The office was in last place in virtually every category. Over the years the branch had a series of poor leaders. Also, there was a very large local competitor who basically owned the neighborhood.

I can still remember facilitating my first all employees meeting. Everyone looked like they had been through a beating. Many of them wouldn't even look up at me while I was talking. The previous Branch Manager was an absolute tyrant who would fire employees for any minor infraction, real or imagined. The employees lived in constant fear of losing their jobs. It was the worst situation I had seen in my career up to that point.

I slowly began to earn the trust of my new employees, but I had to make some tough decisions early on. I demoted two leaders to individual contributor roles and replaced them with strong leaders. I also had to terminate a few severely underperforming employees. In spite of this, I was able to gradually improve the work environment and people began to open up and share ideas on how we could improve our results.

And improve we did! In roughly three years our client satisfaction and retention improved from dead last to right at the overall company average. We began to perform at the level of the typical Branch in these two areas. In my second year employee turnover was cut in half, from around 40% to 20%.

In spite of these successes there was one critical area that never improved: sales. The Sales organization was the only group in my Branch that did not report into me. They faced an impossible competitive situation from a local competitor who owed the market in our territory. This competitor was on the radio and television; they sponsored a local marathon every year. I didn't know how much they spent on marketing and advertising but my marketing budget was simple: zero.

One of the largest factors that Branches were evaluated on was Gross Operating Margin. This number was heavily dependent on Sales. Because sales never rose above 70% of plan, the Branch had not achieved its Gross Operating Margin for at least 10 years. In spite of a revolving door on the Sales leadership side, results never improved. Our corporate office either didn't understand the unique dynamic of having this huge competitor in our backyard, or they didn't care. Their solution was always the same: bring in a new sales leader. It never worked.

So while I improved the areas that I had control over, the sales numbers and top line revenue continued to fall short of plan. Chuck was intelligent enough to understand this dynamic but powerless to affect any real change in strategy. What corporate should have done was compete head-to-head against this competitor in terms of marketing and advertising. We would have eventually worn them out and they quite likely would have sold out to us. Instead, they removed Chuck from his position and had him work on the rollout of a new product. And in came the "hatchet" man.

My fate, and that of two other Branch Managers in the area, was sealed before the new guy ever set foot in any of our Branches. As was always the case at this company, they concluded that if a Branch was missing its operating plan then the solution was to get a new Branch Manager.

My situation was a little different. Our Branch had lost many good employees to this local competitor for more than a decade. So in my case they decided to merge my office with one much further away, thus eliminating my position. I'm sure the thinking was "we'll move the Branch 50 miles from this competitor and make it harder for them to steal our employees." My guess is that this strategy worked.

So in February 2007, for the second time in only five years I found myself out of a job, and now with **three** young children and Cathy still a stay-at-home mom. My accumulated vacation and severance pay would only carry me through early April. And the job situation in Ohio is never great even in a strong economy.

But something had changed in me. I had been through this before and watched God do an amazing miracle, delivering me from unemployment in California just two weeks before my severance and unemployment ran out. I had a much different perspective this time. I even wished the "hatchet" man well after he eliminated my position. From the look on his face I could tell he wasn't expecting that kind of response.

Nonetheless, this was a much more challenging situation as I needed to start a new job in roughly eight weeks. I am convinced that God loves challenging situations because when He cleans them up He gets all the glory. Within 48 hours I received a call from a Sales rep in my old office telling me about an opportunity with a very large, well respected financial services company. She gave me the name of a Sales associate, Perry, who had left my company to work for them. I called Perry and within a couple of days I had a phone interview with the hiring manager. Within two weeks they flew me to New Hampshire and to Dallas for onsite interviews.

The GM for this company's business unit lived in Cincinnati so I met him at a Panera Bread near my home. The GM interview was critical and I knew it. About 30 minutes into our conversation we began discussing my management philosophy. I mentioned that a book I had just read called "Good to Great" by Jim Collins pretty much summed up my leadership philosophy. Well it turned out he had not only read this book but had "dissected" it (his words). This book was basically him game plan for how to run his business unit.

Needless to say I was offered the job! I was paid by my previous company through Friday, 04/06/2007 and started with this new, amazing company on Monday, 04/09/2007! For the second time in five years I had lost my job but not missed a single pay check!

EIGHTEEN

Mark

I've heard many people ask the question "How could a God of love send people to Hell?" The answer is that He doesn't. People send themselves to Hell by rejecting God's free gift of salvation. You have to practically step over Jesus to end up in Hell. God loves everyone and if they seek Him with all their heart the Bible says they will find Him. My life is an example of God pursuing me not once, but twice. This chapter is an interesting example of just how far God will go to get His message to someone, in this case a co-worker and friend of mine named Mark.

I met Mark during my training before I relocated to Cincinnati. He managed the Las Vegas office for my company. We both reported to the same boss, Lynn, in Orange County, California. As part of my training I would fill in for Branch Managers by running their offices when they were on vacation. Mark and I are about the same age and have similar personalities, and we became fast friends.

It became clear that Mark was not a Believer and I prayed for the right opportunity to share my testimony and the gospel with him. Our company had an annual meeting that was a combination of training and fun. The meetings were usually held at a nice resort and we had great speakers. One year the speaker was Frank Abignale, the man featured in the Tom Hanks movie "Catch me if you can." The meeting locations would alternate each year and the events were almost always first class.

At one of my first annual meetings Mark and I were sitting on a patio area with another Branch Manager named Kevin. Kevin managed the Fresno, California office. Lots of free alcohol was provided at these meetings. Mark and Kevin were having a beer and I was just having a Pepsi. As was the case with the last company I had worked for, I was the only person in a leadership position not drinking alcohol. This often gave me an opportunity to share my faith because invariable people would be curious why I wasn't drinking.

Sure enough as we sat there on the patio Kevin starting asking me about why I wasn't having a beer. Finally I had my chance. Just as I was about to take advantage of this great opportunity another Branch Manager showed up at our table and dominated the conversation from that point on. It was so frustrating. I continued to think about this missed opportunity for years.

As you learned in the previous chapter I would eventually lose my job with this company but I still kept in contact with Mark. He earned a promotion and moved his family from Las Vegas to Richmond,

Virginia and ran a much larger office. He called me one day in 2008 saying he was frustrated with the culture at this company where we had both worked. He decided to give his resignation even though he didn't have another job lined up. I didn't tell him this but that sounded like a bad idea. You never want to quit one job without having another one lined up. His decision really surprised me and seemed very out of character for him.

After he left the company the economy started to collapse. Jobs suddenly became very hard to find. I got the feeling Mark was beginning to regret his decision. He called me to see if there were any openings at my company. It turned out that my business unit was expanding our operations to a new office in Albuquerque and we needed a Director out there. I had considered taking the job but changed my mind after visiting the city. It is a run-down, depressing place.

Since Mark was in a precarious situation and really needed a job he interviewed for the position and was hired! I was so excited that once again we were working for the same company, and both reporting to the same boss. He moved his family from Richmond, Virginia to Albuquerque and settled into his new job.

I often traveled to our Hew Hampshire office since most of our employees were located there. I was on the phone one day with Mark and I mentioned an upcoming trip I had planned to New Hampshire. To my surprise he was going to be there the very same week. We decided to get together for dinner during our stay.

We were staying at the same hotel so we drove to a Texas Roadhouse restaurant together. As I was driving to dinner I kept thinking about my missed opportunity from a few years earlier. I was determined not to waste this opportunity. I don't recall how I started the conversation but I spent more than an hour sharing my personal testimony and the gospel with Mark during dinner. He was noncommittal but listened carefully to what I had to say.

A few months later Mark realized that Albuquerque was not a good place to raise a family. He decided to leave our company and take a job in Lexington, Kentucky with a medical company. We only worked together for slightly more than one year. After he left our company I gave some thought to the incredible sequence of events that led to our conversation at the restaurant in New Hampshire. I was amazed at the lengths God went to, providing me a **second** opportunity to have this important conversation with Mark. God was determined that Mark know the truth, and God caused him to do something really crazy, like quit a good job without having another one lined up, in order for this to happen.

Mark called me recently to tell me that his wife and two children just started attending a church in Lexington, Kentucky. It didn't surprise me at all. When I consider how God has pursued Mark, I have no doubt that he will one day say "yes" to Jesus, and pass from death to life.

NINETEEN

Another House Miracle

In the summer of 2007 my new company decided that it made sense to relocate me to Dallas. That was the expansion site at the time for our business unit. Cathy and I hired a wonderful Christian realtor in Cincinnati named Tom Sturm. Tom had been selling homes in our area for 17 years and he was very sharp and professional. However, the numbers he shared with us were not encouraging. Tom said that the Cincinnati real estate market was in the worst shape he had seen in his 17 years in the business. He said that 60% of the listings were eventually being de-listed because the homes didn't sell. He also said that for the homes that did sell, the average time from listing to close was 81 days.

As if these obstacles weren't enough, we had our own challenge to share with Tom. Since it was already mid-summer, we needed a buyer within a couple of weeks and we would probably need a fast escrow, less than the typical 30 days. If this didn't happen we would not make it to Dallas prior to the start of the new school year in August. It seemed pretty hopeless but we all prayed together and asked God for a miracle.

Well that is exactly what God did! Our house sold in exactly seven days and we got 99% of our asking price! It turned out that the new buyer was, like me, going through a corporate relocation, moving from Chicago to Cincinnati. They were in a big hurry also so they asked our realtor if we would be open to an unusually fast escrow of only three weeks!

Something amazing happened during the sales process. The people who ended up buying our house spent almost one hour inspecting our home. While they were walking through our home we were next door at our neighbor's house, spying on them! After they left we walked back to our home and noticed there was a message on our answering machine. It was from our realtor, Tom, saying that he had a second potential buyer who was very interested in our home. This family who ended up making such a quick and strong offer was in our house when Tom's call came through. They would have heard his entire message. As it turned out this second buyer never panned out, but I have no doubt that God had a hand in the timing of that message on our answering machine!

We were just blown away by how God engineered all of this for us! And so was Tom! We said goodbye to the mountains of friends God had given us in Cincinnati and headed for the Lone Star State.

In addition to the two miracles of finding me a new job in only a few weeks and selling our home in seven days, God did one last miracle. When I moved to my new employer my base pay, bonus and benefits were all <u>substantially</u> higher than at my previous company. In fact, the increase in my total compensation package was more than 30%. Employment studies show that most people who lose their jobs take a pay "cut" when they start their new job. What God did was just amazing.

I still have one lingering question. I don't understand why God didn't let me succeed at my job in Cincinnati. He literally put me into an impossible situation, a situation where "no one" could win. Why? What was the purpose for our short three-year stay in Cincinnati? I may never know, but I do know that when God decided my time there was up, He worked out every last detail and delivered me to my next opportunity.

I often wonder how people who do not know Jesus cope with incredibly difficult and emotional situations like the loss of a job. Even with my strong faith and a long history of watching God work many miracles in my life, I still experienced moments of doubt and depression. I remember what it was like to "do life" without God, like I did during my first 14 years of life and during college. It was awful. God's way is so much better. In fact, it's **perfect**.

TWENTY

TCA

We settled into temporary housing in North Dallas while we decided where to send the kids to school and where to live. This was the sequence when we moved to Cincinnati; first find the right Christian school, then buy a house that was close to both my office and the school. Cathy had done a mountain of research on Christian schools and Christian academies in the north Dallas area. To our amazement there were nearly a dozen to choose from, so it was no easy task. She had narrowed it down to two schools, Trinity Christian Academy (TCA) and one other school. We were kind of stuck, not sure which of the two was the "right" school.

One afternoon in early August 2007 we were standing in the parking lot of a hotel where we were staying. We were standing there debating the pros and cons of each school but we couldn't come to a firm decision on either one. We were both very frustrated, more so than at any point since arriving in Dallas. Finding the right Christian school for our three kids was our number one priority, even more important than where we would eventually live.

Just as we were wrapping up our conversation Cathy noticed a young girl behind me and she was walking right toward us. She was wearing a sweatshirt with the letters TCA on the front. Of course Cathy stopped her and asked her what TCA stood for. The young girl told us that it stood for Trinity Christian Academy. Cathy then began to pepper her with questions about TCA.

Well it turned out that this girl was a senior at TCA and had attended school there since kindergarten! She told us that it was an incredible school both academically and spiritually. Cathy asked about the other school we were considering and this girl gave us a laundry list of reasons why she could not recommend it. Well of course that settled it for us! TCA was not <u>our</u> answer, it was <u>God's</u> answer.

That was the "only" time we had a debate about these two schools in a public setting, in this case a parking lot. And what was a high school senior doing in that parking lot in the first place? She must have lived in the area so why would she be at a hotel? And what are the odds of her wearing a TCA sweatshirt that day and walking by us at the exact moment we were having this intense debate? If she had walked by ten minutes earlier of ten minutes later, we never would have met her.

When we as Christians face important and difficult decisions, God will give us the answer. And often times the answer will come in an unexpected way, and through an unexpected person, like a high school senior in a hotel parking lot.

TWENTY ONE

Hearing God Speak

Now that we had the school decision out of the way we moved on to the question of where to live. The very first community we researched was Castle Hills, located about 10 minutes north of the Dallas Fort-Worth airport. Because most of the homes had very small lots and alleyway entrances we passed on this community and then looked literally all over the north Dallas area. It was exhausting.

We leased a house for six months and then moved into a really nice apartment near the airport. They had just added a new section so our apartment was new and we were the first tenants. It had an awesome view of a wetlands area just behind the apartments. I remember us saying that it was probably the nicest view we would ever have out of our dining room window.

After nearly one year of trying to find the right area to live we went back to the first community we had visited, Castle Hills. There was a Dallas area home builder starting a new division and the homes would be in our price range. Their Sales Representative, Jesse, was a Christian and part-time pastor so we felt we would get an honest deal.

The builder made an exception and allowed us to choose a floor plan with a front entry garage. Also, we would be on a cul-de-sac that was shared with just one other home, and we also had a community pool and workout room on our cul-de-sac. Lastly, just like our first home in Chino Hills, California our lot would be more than a ¼ acre, so we would have a large backyard for the kids to play in. It was the perfect house, on the perfect lot and in the perfect community. So in the summer of 2008 we signed a contract.

Cathy is a great negotiator and she was able to secure a huge amount of design center credits for us. She spent countless hours in the summer and fall of 2008 picking out every last detail for our beautiful new home. By the time building was scheduled to begin in early December we had been renting for almost 1.5 years, so we were really anxious to get into a home. Living in an apartment with three high-energy kids was beginning to wear us out.

In mid-November we started hearing rumors that our builder was in financial trouble. The economy was in a free-fall in 2008 and the housing industry was in a mini depression. Small, regional builders like ours were going out of business all over the country. Jesse said he was concerned, and he told us his company had been laying off employees. We had spent so much time and effort on trying to find a home that the thought of starting over was unimaginable.

In late November, just as they were preparing our lot for construction, our builder declared bankruptcy. It was not going to be a reorganization. The company would be liquidated. We were devastated. We were now facing not just the loss of our deposit, but the prospect of having to start all over again after 1.5 years of trying to get into the right house. Cathy and I were completely depressed.

One night a few days after learning about the bankruptcy I woke up around 2:00am and couldn't get back to sleep. I was so stressed out about what had happened. I sat on the floor next to my bed and began pouring out my sadness and frustration to God. Why was this happening? We both thought we had <u>finally</u> found the perfect place to live.

As I sat there silently just wondering what we should do, something happened that I had never experienced in my life, and has never happened since. I heard a voice speak to me so loudly and so clearly that it was as if there was someone sitting right next to me. It was not an "audible" voice, but was as close as you could get to being one.

I don't know if it was the Holy Spirit, God the Father or Jesus who spoke to me, but what He told me was that my thinking about our situation was completely wrong. I was thinking that all of these obstacles meant that things could never work out for this home. God told me that just the opposite was true, that He was going to overcome all of these challenges as proof that this was where he wanted us to live. The voice then quoted a verse from the book of Revelation: "Behold I have set before you an open door that no man can shut."

I was absolutely amazed. As soon as this voice finished speaking to me an indescribable peace came over me. God had just told me that, somehow, in spite of all these challenges, we were going to have this home. For several years we have had a family Bible study with our kids every Sunday night. We switch back and forth between the Old and New Testament. We had just studied the chapter from Revelation that contained the exact verse God had quoted to me! I didn't have any more questions. God had given me the answer and all my anxieties evaporated.

Like I said, this had never happened to me in my life up to that point, and it has never happened since. In the past, there were several times when I had asked God for wisdom in a given situation and He had given me the solution. I remember one time when there was a difficult technical challenge at work that no one could solve. The IT department called a meeting to try and brainstorm for a solution. I was the least technical person invited to the meeting.

About one minute before we got started I prayed and asked God for wisdom. Immediately God put a thought in my mind about how to solve the issue. As soon as the meeting started, I presented my one sentence idea. Everyone got quiet. The systems programmer looked at the applications programmer, who then looked over at his boss. It turned out to be the best answer. It ended up being a very short brainstorming session for the simple reason that God had joined the meeting.

But in this situation and others like it, God didn't have a "conversation" with me. He didn't explain to me why my thinking was completely wrong and then tell me what He was going to do next, and then throw in a Bible verse for good measure! No this time it was completely different and amazing.

The next morning I was up early with our youngest daughter Hannah. She was sick with a bad cough and I was "steaming" her in the bathroom in our apartment. Cathy poked her head into the bathroom and I basically said that the Holy Spirit spoke to me in the middle of the night and told me everything was going to work out on our home. She kind of had this blank stare on her face. She probably thought I was crazy or very sleep deprived.

What happened next was not one miracle but a series of miracles. It turned out that our builder was run by a young man, and his father owned a small home building company in Dallas. The father decided to acquire a few of the contracts written by his son's company and to honor any security deposits. However, he only did this for a handful of homes, ones that had not yet started construction. Only two homes in our neighborhood met these criteria, and our home was one of the two. This new company was actually a high-end builder, so we got a higher quality builder and didn't lose our deposit! Many new homeowners who had recently moved into their homes were sued by sub-contractors who hadn't been paid. It was a real mess but not for us.

They started our home on January 15th 2009, which was Cathy's birthday. Our new builder had scheduled us to close on June 28th, 2009. For some reason I felt like we should move the closing date up a couple of days. I couldn't shake the feeling. I asked the builder and they agreed to move our closing date to June 26th. As a result, we would be able to lock in our interest rate 30 days prior, on May 26th which is my birthday. I certainly didn't plan it that way.

So on May 26th I called our lender and locked in my rate. The very next day mortgage interest rates shot up by almost ½ of one percent. It was one of the largest mortgage rate increases in one day my lender had ever seen. He kept telling me how "lucky" I was to have locked in on May 26th. I of course knew luck had nothing to do with it!

There were so many other amazing things that happened. Our landscaper somehow under-quoted us for an amazing amount of landscaping. When he realized his error he tried to double the price but our new builder made him honor his original price quote. The landscaper also "accidently" made our stone patio and arbor patio much larger than he had planned. God just kept throwing in extra stuff for us! We closed and moved in on June 26th, 2009, almost two years after moving to Dallas.

I have learned that sometimes when God makes us wait for something we need, like a place to live, He often blesses us with more than we could imagine. That was truly the case with our home in Dallas, Texas. As strange as it might sound, I would absolutely go through all of this difficulty again just for the chance to hear God speak to me in such an amazing way. For those who have experienced this during times of great distress there are no words to describe how incredible it is!

TWENTY TWO

Almost Losing Cathy

In the spring of 2010 we were reaching the end of the road financially in terms of paying for the tuition at TCA. We realized that Cathy would need to begin looking for a job. She enrolled in and completed a Texas accreditation program for teaching and began applying for jobs in both the public and private sector. As Cathy had been a stay-at-home mom since Lauren was born this was creating a lot of stress for both of us. It would be a huge adjustment not having Cathy at home.

It was during this stressful time that Cathy noticed some red dots on her body. At first there were only a handful so we weren't concerned. I thought it might be related to the stress she was experiencing. However, within a few days there were many more and she had a terrible pain in her throat that was preventing her from eating. As a result of not being able to eat she started to become very weak.

Our family physician told us she needed to go to the ER. I drove her to the emergency room at Plano Presbyterian Hospital, about ten minutes from our home. I began thinking "not another trial God!" We had barely gotten settled into our new home and now this.

The hospital decided to admit her and then began running a series of tests. They couldn't seem to find out what was wrong and Cathy kept getting worse every day. She soon developed a high fever. At first they thought she might have a very bad case of the chicken pox, but they weren't sure. All of the tests kept coming back negative. By her fifth day in the hospital I began to think she might not make it. She told me weeks later that she felt the same thing on that day. Cathy was dying.

I just couldn't believe this was happening. How could I lose her now? How could I possibly raise three children on my own? Every morning before calling her I would hope and pray that she had a good night's sleep and that she was feeling better. Every morning my spirits would drop as she told me she was getting worse.

I decided against her wishes to have Cathy's parents fly out from California. She was concerned that if it truly was chicken pox that she could infect them, at their age it could be fatal. My thought was that if Cathy died and her parents weren't there by her side, they would be devastated. We had her parents wear masks while in the room with her just to be safe.

Our children's school, TCA, has a process for informing other TCA parents when a child or parent is seriously ill. On Cathy's second day in the hospital they began sending out prayer requests for Cathy to other TCA parents via e-mail. Many parents, faculty and staff members began praying for her. TCA parents were wonderful to us. They brought us enough food to feed an army. Parents picked up our kids from school and in some cases kept them overnight. In spite of all this help, my life felt like complete chaos.

We were serving in the children's ministry at church so some of the pastors and staff from church were also praying for her. One of the community pastors came to see Cathy and prayed for her while I was there. There were hundreds of Believers praying for her. In order for Cathy to be discharged from the hospital we needed two things to happen: her fever had to go away and she needed to be able to eat on her own. During her seventh night in the hospital, God healed her and she was able to come home.

I now had come close to losing both my son and my wife. God had come through for us again. The hospital was never able to determine the cause of her illness, so they never implemented a treatment plan other than antibiotics. Cathy went to several specialists after she was discharged but finally gave up when none could tell her what had caused the illness. She still has a relapse every few months but nothing as severe as the original illness.

Cathy - They said it might be chicken pox but it became my "thorn in the flesh." I developed red sores on my back and inside my mouth and throat. To numb the pain of having sores inside my mouth and throat, the doctors gave me very strong pain medications that knocked me out within a few seconds of it being injected into my IV. I slept through most of my eight day hospital stay. When I was awake, it was lonely and depressing being in the hospital. Everything looked gray and colorless outside my window.

By the time I was admitted to the hospital, I hadn't eaten or had much to drink for the past two weeks. Because it was so excruciatingly painful to swallow I basically stopped eating and drinking. Now that I was in the hospital the IV kept me going. But I still had no appetite. I'd lost almost 15 lbs. This was not exactly the ideal weight loss program.

By the fifth day of being in the hospital with no improvement, I became very depressed. I seriously thought I would die that week. I was frantic when two pastors showed up on the same day to anoint me with oil and pray with me. I thought for sure I was dying and that they were giving me my last rites but not telling me the truth about the seriousness of my illness. It turned out the pastors heard I was sick and cared enough to visit me at the hospital.

When everyone left that evening, I was depressed. I decided to have a heart to heart talk with God. I knew Jesus sat at the foot of my bed that night as I poured out my heart to Him. I was ready to die and meet Him in Heaven but I was concerned about leaving Duane and my three children. If He wanted me to stay on earth, I promised God that I would raise my children to know and serve Him. I hadn't done a good enough job of raising Godly children so I asked if He would allow me to live a bit longer so I could finish the job well. It was the closest I ever felt to Jesus. I really believe I was at the door to eternity that night.

TWENTY THREE

Thuzie

When our son Ryan was born in 1999 we sold our Toyota Camry and purchased a new Toyota Sienna. This made life so much easier since at the time we had a newborn and a two year old. By the spring of 2011 our van was 12 years old and had 170,000 miles on it. There were a couple of places where it was literally held together with tape. We could not afford a new car so we just kept driving our van, hoping it wouldn't die on us. At some point in 2009 we actually gave our van the name Thuzie, which was short for Methuselah, the oldest person who ever lived in the Old Testament! Given how old our van was getting we decided it was a fitting name!

In March of 2011 my company increased the grade level for my position, and also increased my bonus percentage. It was totally unexpected. The monthly increase in my pay was just over $400. The very next month Cathy had just dropped the kids off to school when Thuzie started smoking. The smoke was so bad that it began filling the van with smoke. Cathy called me on her cell phone in a panic. She said she was driving to our mechanic's shop. I told her that if it looked like Thuzie was catching on fire to pull off the road and get out as fast as she could.

Just as she pulled Thuzie into the driveway of our mechanic Thuzie breathed her last. She died right there in their driveway. The mechanic did some checking and told us a new engine would cost around $8,000. Given Thuzie's age we wisely choose to sell her to the junk yard for $500. Seeing her taken away was a little bit emotional for us. All three of our children had sort of grown up in Thuzie. She had even survived missionary trips to small rural villages in Mexico. Now she was gone and we needed to find another car.

Cathy had always wanted a Toyota Sequoia and we found one at a Ford dealership near our home. It was used but had low mileage. When I checked the Kelly Blue Book for this same car I noticed that the Ford Dealership had listed this Sequoia "below" low blue book. Given the great price I guessed it would have some type of damage. We went down to look it over and found that it was in really good shape. Cathy is a great negotiator and she started to work them on the price. I had forgotten to tell her that their price was already below the low Kelly Blue Book price. The Sales guy clearly hadn't checked this when they priced the vehicle, because he went online to check after Cathy asked for a better price.

I could see the surprised look on his face when he discovered what I already knew, that they had priced the car well below market. He quickly hardened his position. There would be no negotiating. I gladly accepted the car as is and we took it home. We did not have the money to pay for the car but we got a great interest rate on the loan. Our monthly payment would be just over $400 per month, the amount of the increase in my pay that occurred the month before.

What's interesting is that I didn't tie these two events together until months later. When it hit me I was once again amazed by God's perfect timing. He knew of course that we didn't have the money for a car payment, so He provided it first and **then** let Thuzie breath her last. God's timing is always perfect.

TWENTY FOUR

A Tuition Miracle

I mentioned earlier that the large profit we made selling our California home in 2004 had been paying for Christian school tuition for many years. Well by 2010 this money had run out. We began to use some retirement savings while we figured out what to do. My income would cover all of our living expenses but there was nothing left over for the annual tuition bill of roughly $45,000. It was a mountain for us. We decided that in order for Lauren, Ryan and Hannah to continue attending TCA Cathy would have to go back to work. Cathy had been a stay-at-home mom for almost 15 years. Finding a job that, after taxes, would cover a $45,000 tuition bill seemed next to impossible.

In the summer of 2011 Cathy began applying for various jobs. To our surprise she was invited to interview with several companies and by late summer got her first job offer. Unfortunately, the pay was not enough to cover the full tuition expense but we felt she should take the job. About a week after she started working we happened to be eating at our favorite Asian food restaurant near our church. When Cathy opened her fortune cookie it said "You will give up the smaller one for the larger one." It was a very strange and specific message.

A week later Cathy received a job offer from a very large company called Thomson Reuters. The hiring manager never even met with her in person. He offered her a job that was less than one mile from the TCA campus, and the after-tax amount would completely cover the tuition for all three of our kids! Needless to say, she resigned from the "smaller" one and went to work for the "larger" one. I'm convinced that God has a sense of humor!

Given that Cathy had not been in the work force for 15 years, it didn't make any sense for someone to offer her a position with such a high salary. Not only was the salary perfect, but since her office was only one mile from school she could drop the kids off and be at work in less than five minutes. The after school pickup was equally convenient.

Just for fun I took Cathy's ending salary from 15 years earlier. I then did some math assuming she had earned the typical merit increase every year for 15 years. The ending salary was almost exactly equal to her starting salary at Thomson Reuters. Do you see what God did? God honored our decision to have her stay home while our children were young. From a financial stand point, it was like she never left the work force. She picked up right where she left off! And God waited to send her back to work until our youngest child Hannah entered Kindergarten.

Back in 1997 when we decided to have Cathy stay home with Lauren, the math didn't work at all. But that was "our" math. God is not constrained by our math. He is not limited in what He can do. If you are facing the same decision and you feel it is what God wants for your family, then step out in faith. You'll be amazed at the miracles He will accomplish in your life. Where God leads God provides.

TWENTY FIVE

Mom & Dad

My mom was born in Evansville, Arkansas and grew up in Stillwell, Oklahoma. She was the oldest of six children. None of her family members were Christians and they never attended church. Because she grew up during the Great Depression her family was extremely poor. Since she was the oldest child my mom had to begin cooking for the family when she was around 10 years old. It was a hard life.

During World War II some missionaries came to her public school and shared the gospel with the students. Given our culture today it's hard to imagine this happening, but in those days it was common. On her way home from school that day my mom stopped by a small pond and gave her life to Jesus. She was 11 years old at the time.

My mom never wavered in her faith and made sure my siblings and I knew and understood the Bible. She had a passion for child evangelism and held regular "good news" clubs for the kids in our neighborhood. My mom was one of the kindest people I have ever known. I never heard her say an unkind word about anyone. My mom was the only person in this world who ever loved me unconditionally. She was a true Saint.

In 1992, the year Cathy and I were married, my mom began having unusual symptoms. Her energy level was low so they thought it might be a thyroid issue. Then she had difficulty standing and had to use a cane, even though she was only 61 years old at the time. For a period of several months various tests were run to determine the cause of her illness. This was such a stressful time for me because of my close relationship with her.

Finally the diagnosis came in and it was devastating. Mom had Lou Gehrig's disease, known officially as Amyotrophic Lateral Sclerosis or ALS. Basically the brain is unable to transmit messages to the muscles, so over time they atrophy. Patients slowly lose their strength, and some can end up completely paralyzed. There is no cure for ALS and it is always fatal. Mom was handed a death sentence.

When I heard the news I felt like the wind had been knocked out of me. I was only 27 years old. How could I lose this woman who meant so much to me? I went into our downstairs guest bathroom, turned on the fan and cried for a very long time.

Around that same time I learned that my dad had Hepatitis C. This is also incurable and eventually destroys the liver, leading to death. I began praying for God to heal my parents, mom of her ALS and dad of his Hepatitis C. I'll be honest and admit that my prayers for my mom were fervent and heart-felt. I just didn't have the same level of compassion for my dad.

Over the next several years my mom's condition continued to worsen. By 1997 she had to have a motorized wheelchair to move around her home. Her strength was fading. By early 1999 she had to have an oxygen tank in order to get enough air. In late December of 1999 I received the call I had been dreading. Mom had been taken to a small hospital near her home and she was in really bad shape. She was transferred to a larger hospital and moved to a wing for the terminally ill.

My oldest sister Donna and I stayed up with her all night, talking to her and holding her hands. Mom asked us to sing several of her favorite hymns. I couldn't remember very many of the words to these old hymns but I did the best I could. It's strange the things you notice when you are spending your last few hours with someone you love so much. I noticed her hands. As I held them I noticed how small they were. These hands that had raised me, that had rocked me to sleep and fed me. This wonderful, loving Godly woman was leaving me. It broke my heart.

Mom went to Heaven the next day. Although I had grieved for her condition for seven years, when she finally passed away an amazing peace came over me. Her pain was gone. Not just the physical pain, but the emotional pain from a very difficult marriage to a man who never showed love to any of us. Mom was home and I was completely at peace. I still miss her and think about her often but I don't sorrow as those who have no hope. We will be together again one day, and when that happens I'll never have to worry about losing her again.

A couple of years after mom died my dad told me that a blood test revealed he had been completely healed of Hepatitis C. This isn't supposed to happen. Once you have it you have it for life. It was clearly a medical miracle. I didn't say this to my dad but my obvious question to God was "Why?" Why did you heal dad instead of mom? I needed my mom, and dad was just a source of never ending irritation. It didn't make any sense. But as I thought about the joy my mom was experiencing in Heaven I came to terms with it. God did heal mom, permanently, by taking her home.

My dad lived for seven years after my mom died and passed away in September of 2006. My four siblings and I went to stay with him a few days before he died. Once again it was my sister Donna and I who sat by his side, engaging him in conversation. His other children and grandchildren sat in the other room watching movies from Blockbuster. It was surreal. Here was my dad, dying in the family room while almost everyone else watched the latest version of King Kong in the living room. I guess it made sense.

My dad never got to know any of us, never invested time in us. So why would they want to start a relationship with him now. It was so incredibly sad.

The last words I said to my dad were "I love you dad." His response was "I love all you kids." Even on his death bed he couldn't say "I love you" for the simple reason that it wasn't true. I sincerely hope my dad made it into Heaven. Only God knows for sure.

TWENTY SIX

The Peace of God

In the very beginning of this book I mentioned that there were two things that prompted me to write this book. One was that my oldest daughter Lauren had just started high school and would leave for college in four years. The other was a very difficult trial I was going through at work.

The daily stress created by the situation at work was almost unbearable. Barely a few hours would go by without me thinking about it. I would think about it even on the weekends. It was beginning to affect my health and my overall mental state. After seven months I had reached a point where I told God that I couldn't go on like this. If this didn't end soon this trial was going to destroy me in some way, perhaps physically. It was awful.

One Saturday morning I was driving alone doing some errands. As usual I was thinking about the mess at work when suddenly all of my fear and anxiety just evaporated. It all happened in a split second. I felt a complete peace come over me. It was like someone had flipped a switch in my brain and I was no longer capable of experiencing any stress about my situation. I was stunned. This had never happened to me before.

During past trials the difficulty would eventually end and I would gradually begin to feel better emotionally and mentally. This was completely different. My circumstances hadn't changed but now I felt nothing but peace.

In the first few days after this happened I thought it would be temporary. In fact, at one point I actually tried to "force" myself to feel stressed out again but I couldn't. God had given me His peace and it was permanent. It couldn't be undone. It was all so strange and amazing. I think God knew that if He didn't intervene I would have ended up with cancer. I discovered recently that I have stomach ulcers, no doubt related to this seven-month nightmare. It could have been much worse.

As the result of several very unlikely events, the situation resolved itself. So like all previous trials in my life, this one ended. To me the amazing part of this story is not that God delivered me from yet another trial. He has always delivered me. What amazed me was how He completely removed the mental and emotional damage being done to me by the trial. And He did this in an instant on that Saturday afternoon. It was totally unexpected.

In I Corinthians 10:13 God promises He will never allow us to be tested beyond what we are able to endure. God knew that seven months was all I could take so He flipped a switch and replaced my anxiety with His complete peace. And He did it without my even asking. And He can do the same for you.

TWENTY SEVEN

When Miracles Don't Happen

Our move to Dallas was difficult because we had to leave behind so many wonderful friends in Cincinnati. For the second time in three years we had to start over, as we had no friends or family members living in Dallas. We knew that we wanted to have a dog for the kids so a few weeks after we were settled into our home in Dallas we visited a local animal shelter. I took the kids with me but not Cathy.

After searching for a while Lauren noticed a small dog that looked like a Pomeranian. It turned out he was a mix Pomeranian – Sheepdog. He really perked up when we spotted him so we took him outside to spend some time with him. I had a feeling this might be the right dog for us. I remember he whined (cried) loudly when Lauren and Ryan left him.

Back at home I asked Cathy to visit the shelter with me to get her opinion. She agreed with Lauren that this little guy was the one. He was about three months old and had been found wondering the streets in a local city called Irving. He didn't have a collar or micro-chip so he ended up at the shelter. We would soon discover that he had a bad habit of trying to escape, which is probably why his first owner lost him.

He came home with us in the summer of 2009, right after we moved into our new home. We weren't sure what to name him. At first we tried "Dallas" but that didn't seem to fit. At the shelter they called him Prince but we didn't like that name. Lauren got the bright idea to call him "Mason", the name of the city we lived in back in Cincinnati. Strangely enough he responded to this name immediately. We had found the right name for him.

Since all of our three kids were in school and Cathy was still a stay-at-home mom, Mason and Cathy became best friends. He would literally follow Cathy around from room to room in our house. He bonded with her immediately. When she would sit at the table and read or work on the computer, Mason would be right there under her feet. When she was in our room and he couldn't get in, he would sit by the door and cry.

Every time I would come home from work you would think I had been gone for a month based on the reception Mason would give me at the garage door. Mason was a huge comfort to Cathy in those first couple of years. His presence and loyalty would lift her spirits when she was lonely. Mason was a huge blessing to all of us, a true little "Hachi". He was perfect.

Mason had two bad habits. He was an escape artist and he ate everything in sight. He would eat paper, cardboard, toys, anything left on the floor. Because of this we developed elaborate safety procedures to prevent escapes and to prevent him from eating anything truly dangerous. In spite of this he managed to escape at least seven times. We always caught up with him and brought him back home. His droppings in the back yard revealed his success at thwarting our efforts to keep him from eating anything other than food.

Three days after Christmas 2012 Mason began vomiting. Within 24 hours it became clear that he was in real trouble and so we took him to an emergency pet hospital near our home. An X-ray revealed he had swallowed something very large and that it was lodged in his intestines. Without immediate surgery he wouldn't live. In all honesty we didn't have the money for surgery. However, given how much he meant to Cathy and to my oldest daughter Lauren, I agreed to let them operate on him.

They found and removed a small rubber duck. He must have snuck into one of the bathrooms when we weren't looking and swallowed it whole. They told us that there was major damage to areas of his intestines that are very critical. They suggested he might need a second, more expensive operation by a board certified surgeon. We knew that this was not an option for us financially.

Since he was scheduled to spend another 24 hours in the hospital we asked them to try and feed him with a tube through his nose. Our plan was to pick him up the next morning and nurse him back to health at home. During the entire ordeal we prayed diligently for Mason and asked God to perform a miracle and heal him. He was such an important member of our family, having lived with us for over three years.

Early the next morning around 3:30am we got a call saying that Mason was in bad shape. It appeared that his intestines had ruptured, possibly due to the nutrition provided by the feeding tube. He wasn't going to live much longer. They asked us to come in to say goodbye. We were devastated. Cathy, Lauren and I were heart broken.

Lauren and I drove to the hospital and spent a few minutes kissing him and saying our goodbyes. The doctor gave him an injection and he died quietly in our arms. On the drive back home Lauren and I both cried the whole way and she said to me through her tears "Dad, God just took my best friend from me."

I am writing this account the day Mason passed away. He died just eight hours ago. So my question to God is "Why"? Given how much he meant to our family, why did God allow this to happen? Why didn't God perform a miracle and heal him after his operation? Why was Mason taken from us in the prime of his life?

As we sit here at home today mourning his passing we don't have any answers. We don't know why. We might never completely understand this. But we do know this. God loves us, and he also loved Mason more than we ever could. If He allowed our hearts to break this week it was for a reason. And we need to keep trusting Him, even when He "doesn't" perform the miracles we ask Him for.

TWENTY EIGHT

Meddling

Our family attends a wonderful church in Carrollton Texas called Bent Tree Bible Fellowship. Our pastor, Pete Briscoe, is one of the best expositional Bible teachers in the country. His teaching is straightforward and he provides a practical application at the end of most messages. He sometimes warns us as he begins the "application" phase of his message that he is moving "from preaching to meddling". This is when he addresses the "so what?" or "now what?" questions. My guess is that this is the point in his sermons where some people begin to get a little uncomfortable.

I hope you found the previous 27 chapters interesting or even inspiring, but I have to warn you that the rest of this book falls into the category of "meddling". I want you to consider how the truths mentioned here apply to you. Like Pastor Pete, I want to be honest about what's coming next. I hope you'll keep reading.

If you are a parent who has been walking with the Lord for any length of time then I know with certainty you have your own list of the amazing things God has done in your life and in the life of your family. It is so important that you share these experiences with your children. I encourage you to write them down and then spend an evening discussing the list with your kids. Although they might think it's awkward, especially if you have teenagers, hearing the practical ways that God has worked in your life will have a lasting impact on them. They won't be able to dismiss what you share as just some story about people they will never know. It will be about your life and, by extension, their lives as well. I wish my parents had done this in our family but they never did.

As I think about my life so far I realize it is a story of God pursuing me, twice. It is a story of God's faithfulness and provision, of Him "working all things together for good." Some of the trials were my own making, based on really stupid decisions on my part. Others were not. I certainly did not do anything to cause both my son and my wife to become gravely ill. However, in either case, whether self-inflicted or seemingly random, God intervened and in ways that were so improbable that the circumstances could only be described as miracles.

Just because we are Believers we are not exempted from trials. In fact, James says in chapter one of the book that bears his name that we are to "Count it all joy when we fall into various trials, knowing that the testing of our faith produces patience. But let patience have its perfect work, that you may be perfect and complete, lacking nothing." So what he is saying is that we can't achieve completeness in our Christian lives without trials.

Trials don't make us or break us. They simply reveal our level of maturity as Christians. So ask yourself, how do I respond when each new trial arrives in my life? Do I whine, complain and ask God why He has allowed suffering in my life? Think about the book of Job in the Old Testament. Job lost his children, his life savings and his health all at the same time. And how did Job respond? He responded by worshiping! "Then Job tore his robe, and shaved his head, and fell to the ground and **worshipped**." Job 1:20. I am amazed by this. And I also know that my maturity as a Christian is nowhere near what Job had achieved. Having lost my job twice, my first thought as I was driving home was definitely not to "worship"; it was to "worry".

Intellectually we know that anything we would consider negative that happens in our lives must first be allowed by God. He essentially "filters" the events that happen to us, denying some and allowing others. That is exactly what happened with Job. God allowed Satan to afflict Job but only up to a point. The same is true for us. God sets a limit on the trials in our lives, never tests us beyond what we are able to endure, and then works all things together for good. So it should be easy to "count it all joy" every time that new trial arrives. But it's not. I'm not there yet but I have a few years ahead of me so hopefully one day I'll respond the way Job did, with "worship".

I have often wondered how my life would have been different if I had not made so many poor decisions. Did God intend all along for us to move to Ohio and then to Texas, or were we supposed to remain in Southern California our entire lives? Of course there is no way to know. I have often found it almost maddening trying to figure things like this out.

I recently found a verse in Proverbs that reminded me that this effort is a waste of time. Proverbs 20:24 reads, "A man's steps are directed by the Lord. How then can anyone understand his own way." So the answer is simple, we can't! Our lives take unexpected turns that seemingly make no sense to us at the time. We second guess ourselves. We wonder what would have happened if only we had made a different or "better" decision. It can make us crazy.

But we need to remember that God's ways are not our ways. Isaiah 55:9 says, "For as the heavens are higher than the earth, so are My ways higher than your ways, and My thoughts than your thoughts." How can we possibly figure God out? We can't. We are so limited in our thinking, and God is infinite and eternal.

The Apostle Paul may have struggled with this when he said in Philippians chapter 3: "Forgetting those things which are behind and reaching forward to those things which are ahead." I'm sure Paul had more reason to regret his past decisions than most of us. He was responsible for the imprisonment and death of many believers. My guess is that he fell into the same trap we do by second guessing and wondering "what if" or "if only I had".

The bottom line is that we are not God, so we are not capable of figuring out why our lives have played out the way they have. The key is to focus on those things which are ahead. Don't look back, look forward. God has lots for you to do tomorrow and every day after that.

I've heard people say that they look forward to getting to Heaven so they can get all of their questions answered. They will finally know why things played out the way they did in this life. I don't think we'll care once we get to Heaven. In fact, the Bible says in Isaiah 65:17 "For, behold, I create new heavens and a new earth: and the former shall not be remembered, nor come into mind."

To be honest when I get to Heaven I don't want to remember much of what I've written in this book. And I don't think I will, given this passage from Isaiah. We can't completely figure out God. We won't understand the reasons why God allowed certain things to happen to us in this life. But the good news is that when we get to our "permanent" home we won't care. In fact, we won't even remember that we once wanted to know.

TWENTY NINE

The Fall of Work

Writing this first book has caused me to imagine another five or six books I'd like to write. One book I'd love to write would be titled "The Fall of Work". Many of the life challenges described in this book are related to work. We read in Genesis Chapter three that Adam and Eve's sin resulted in the following negative consequences:

- The serpent was cursed
- Creation was put under a curse
- The pain of child bearing was greatly increased
- There would now be conflict in the marriage relationship
- Work was made much more difficult

Here is what God declared: Then to Adam He said, "Because you have heeded the voice of your wife, and have eaten from the tree of which I commanded you, saying, 'You shall not eat of it': "Cursed is the ground for your sake. In toil you shall eat of it all the days of your life. Both thorns and thistles it shall bring forth for you, and you shall eat the herb of the field. In the sweat of your face you shall eat bread until you return to the ground."

Before he sinned Adam had it pretty easy. All he had to do was "tend the garden". Now work was going to be one huge pain in the neck.

Studies show that the majority of workers are dissatisfied with their jobs and that, at any given time, roughly 25% are actively looking for another job. A typical U.S. employee will work for several different companies in their lifetime and most will experience at least one layoff. None of this is a surprise to anyone who has been working for any length of time.

How many people do you know who describe how wonderful their work environment is year after year? How many people do you know who "always" get that big promotion, who only have satisfied clients and whose bosses are completely fair and unbiased? How many companies consistently exceed their financial goals year after year?

The truth is work is riddled with setbacks and disappointments. There are certainly some mountain top experiences along the way: A great sales year or a big promotion from time to time, but these are the exceptions and not the rule. And they are inevitably followed quickly by challenges. Think about all of the business books out there. They are filled with examples of business failures, and advice on how to achieve better results.

So here's the interesting thing. I had read the book of Genesis dozens of times and somehow I'd missed this part about work falling under a curse. This all hit me about a dozen years after finishing college. I had been reflecting not just on my own challenges at work but those of so many of my friends and family members. Everyone I knew had depressing stories about horrific bosses, nightmare employees, difficult and demanding clients, failed business strategies, layoffs, workplace harassment and even workplace violence. The list was endless. Adam had "wrecked" work for every person who would follow after him.

Surprisingly, making this realization made me feel better. For one thing, everyone was in the same boat. No one is exempt from "the fall of work". Also, this caused me to realize that the never ending challenges at work were not because I wasn't working hard enough or smart enough. Understanding this helped me in some small way to cope with all of the difficulties at work. I hope this realization will help you as well.

Thankfully there is some "good" news related to work and these other areas that are under a curse. When Jesus returns to the Earth at the end of the Tribulation, He will establish His kingdom here for 1,000 years. During that time all of these curses will be removed. I can't wait!

THIRTY

Passing the Test

As I mentioned before, the New Testament book of James tells us to "Count it all joy when you fall into various trials, knowing that the testing of your faith produces patience." God allows these "tests" in our lives but never gives us more than we can handle. However, the only way to avoid having to retake a particular test is to pass it. Sometimes I fail a specific type of test and so God puts me right back through that same trial again.

I have a Christian relative who absolutely causes me to lose my mind. This person has a personality very similar to my dad's, so when I'm around this person I just lose it. I have failed this test every single time. If fact, my grades are actually getting worse, not better. So guess what God is going to do? He's going to keep putting me through the ringer until I respond to this person the way He would respond, with love, grace and mercy. Until then I'll have to keep taking this one over and over again.

As we pass these various tests that God allows in our lives our faith increases. I am beginning to understand just how important faith is to God. In first Peter 1:6-7 we read "In this you greatly rejoice, though now for a little while, if need be, you have been grieved by various trials, that the genuineness of your faith, being much more precious than gold that perishes, though it is tested by fire, may be found to praise, honor, and glory at the revelation of Jesus Christ." Do you see how much value God places on our faith? It's not during the good times that we grow our faith, it's during the trials. And the great news is that God promises in 1 Corinthians 10:13 to never test us beyond what we are able to endure. I don't know how many more years it will take but I hope that one day before I leave this life I'll be able to pass this particular test that I've failed so many times in the past.

In the Old Testament book of Jeremiah we read, "The word which came to Jeremiah from the LORD, saying: "Arise and go down to the potter's house, and there I will cause you to hear My words." Then I went down to the potter's house, and there he was, making something at the wheel. And the vessel that he made of clay was marred in the hand of the potter; so he made it again into another vessel, as it seemed good to the potter to make."

In order for the potter to create the pottery, the clay has to remain right in the center of the wheel. In this passage from Jeremiah Israel was the clay, and because they had rebelled against God, disaster was heading their way. We as Christians are like the potter's clay. When we resist the pressure that God allows in our lives and take matters into our own hands, we fall flat on our faces and make a complete mess of things. Then God picks us up, puts us back on the center of the wheel and starts working on us again.

God continues this process for as long as He keeps us here on the Earth. So what is the ultimate purpose of this sometimes painful process? I believe the answer is found in Romans 8:29: "For whom He foreknew, He also predestined to be conformed to the image of His Son." God's goal for every believer on the planet is the same, to make us look, act and think more like Jesus. It's that simple. If you are more like Jesus today than you were last month or last year, then you're on the right track. But we can't get there without pressure, without these occasional trials that God allows in our lives.

Think about the times when you grew the most in your relationship with the Lord. When did you experience the biggest increases in your faith? It was certainly not during the good times, when everything was going your way. No, it was during times of great trials and testing. You see God knows that as Christians we have a tendency to get "soft" and to even backslide when times are good. Think about David. He didn't commit his greatest sins while fleeing from King Saul. It was when things were going well, during a time when he decided to stay home from battle.

So when you're being tested, when God starts applying some pressure, pray and ask Him what He wants to teach you. And never let a trial go to waste!

The Not-So-Secret Formula

When I think back over my life so far, I realize that while I have had plenty of financial **stress**, I have not had actual financial **hardship**. For example, even though I have been unemployed twice for a total of seven months, I have never been without a pay check. In fact, during those periods of unemployment I actually made more money because I was receiving unemployment benefits in addition to my regular pay check. God has always provided for me and my family in abundance. Why?

I believe the answer is found in Malachi chapter 3. Here is what it says: "Will a man rob God? Yet you have robbed Me! But you say, 'In what way have we robbed You?' In tithes and offerings. You are cursed with a curse, for you have robbed Me, even this whole nation. Bring all the tithes into the storehouse, that there may be food in My house, and **try Me** now in this," Says the Lord of hosts, "If I will not open for you the windows of heaven and pour out for you such blessing that there will not be room enough to receive it."

This is the only place in the Bible where God challenges us as Believers to "try Him", or "put Him to the test". It is clear from this passage of scripture that if we will be faithful in our tithes and offerings that God will in turn bless us so abundantly that there will not be room enough to receive it. I believe that the reason I have never struggled financially is because I have remained faithful in my tithes and offerings.

In the first year I became a Christian I felt God wanted me to give away $30.00, which on that day in 1980 was all the money I had. I don't remember who I gave it to, but since I felt strongly that it was what God wanted me to do I gave it away. The very next week a letter arrived in the mail from a Christian camp where I had worked on several occasions as a counselor. About a month earlier I had gotten sick the very day I was scheduled to begin a new week as a camp counselor. I ended up not working that week. Well the letter contained a check for $30.00, the amount they would pay each camp counselor. Even though I was too sick to work they decided to go ahead and pay me any way.

This was an important early lesson for me as a new Christian. God certainly didn't need my $30.00. Even way back in 1980 it wasn't a lot of money. But He did need to teach me a lesson in obedience. And when I obeyed, He then demonstrated for me how easy it was for Him to restore to me what I'd given away. I've always remembered that first test and it greatly impacted my perspective on giving.

When I was unemployed the first time in 2002, I was tempted to stop tithing. After all, I didn't have a job. But I quickly decided that as long as I had a paycheck coming in I was going to keep tithing. When we ran out of money for school tuition and were taking money out of retirement savings to cover the bills, I was again tempted to stop tithing, but I didn't.

Some Christians will argue that tithing only applies to the Old Testament and that since we are no longer under the Law it doesn't apply to us today. This is not what the Bible teaches. The Law was given by God through Moses. More than 400 years **before** Moses ever lived Abraham tithed to a mysterious person called Melchizedek. Many Bible scholars believe that Melchizedek is none other than Jesus Himself. Jesus showed up several times in the Old Testament. But the point is tithing **predated** the Law by more than 400 years.

In Matthew 23:23 Jesus said, "Woe to you, scribes and Pharisees, hypocrites! For you pay tithe of mint and anise and cummin, and have neglected the weightier matters of the law: justice and mercy and faith. These you ought to have done, without leaving the others undone." What a great opportunity for Jesus to say something like "don't you know that tithing was part of the Law and you are no longer under the Law!" But He didn't! He said just the opposite, that these (tithing) "you ought to have done".

147

God has laid down a very simple principle for Believers and it is timeless. The first 10% of what He gives us belongs to Him. And if we will be faithful in this area he will pour out a huge blessing on us. The blessing will not always be financial, but it will be a blessing.

One of my close Christian friends in Southern California would always complain about how something would break or go wrong every month, costing him several hundred dollars each time. At one point I decided to ask him about his tithing. He said that he didn't tithe from his income but he tithed of his "time" to God. My Christian friend was essentially robbing God and you can't get away with this if you are a true Believer. You'll end up paying your tithe anyway by paying for a broken washer or refrigerator, and you will completely miss out on the blessing God has for you.

I'm not saying it's easy to be faithful in your tithes and offering. It's not. Many Christians think "How can I give to God when I can barely pay the bills." The fact is there is a very good chance that the reason they are having trouble paying the bills is because they are robbing God of what belongs to Him. God's formula is so incredibly simple and His promise is so amazing! So my advice is to take God up on His word and "try Him". He won't disappoint you.

If you do decide to put God to the test in the area of tithing there is a second part to the formula, and it has to do with your motives. In 2 Corinthians 9:7 we read "So let each one give as he purposes in his heart, not grudgingly or of necessity; for God loves a cheerful giver." If while you are tithing you are moaning, groaning and complaining, then don't give! God doesn't need your money. He owns everything. His resources are unlimited and He will simply accomplish His purposes through someone else. But remember that "someone else" will then receive God's blessing, not you.

A third part of the formula is found in Matthew Chapter 6: 1-4: "Take heed that you do not do your charitable deeds before men, to be seen by them. Otherwise you have no reward from your Father in heaven. Therefore, when you do a charitable deed, do not sound a trumpet before you as the hypocrites do in the synagogues and in the streets, that they may have glory from men. Assuredly, I say to you, they have their reward. But when you do a charitable deed, do not let your left hand know what your right hand is doing, that your charitable deed may be in secret; and your Father who sees in secret will Himself reward you openly."

I had a firsthand experience with this on one of my short-term mission trips. There were 20 of us traveling from Los Angeles to Moscow. Since we came from different churches we didn't all know each other very well. We all met at the airport and while we were waiting to board our flight another team member whom I had not met came up and introduced herself to me. I was 30 at the time and she was probably around age 60.

After some brief small talk she immediately launched into a laundry list of all the amazing things she had done for God. She even said that one of her projects was mentioned by her pastor in a recent service. I had never heard such blatant boasting by a Christian and I was really bothered by it. Didn't she know that every time she boasted about her charitable deeds she was lighting a fire that would one day consume any reward she might have earned? I wanted to say to her "don't you know what the Bible says in Matthew Chapter 6 about doing you works to be seen by men!"

Well because she was so much older than me I didn't say anything to her. I just smiled and nodded. I think the saddest part in this story is that this woman had already lived most of her life and she never figured it out, she never understood God's precepts. You've heard the saying "forgive and forget." Well when it coming to your tithes and offerings, the best strategy is to "give and forget", and keep it between you and the Lord.

There is another thing I've discovered over the years and it has to do with blessings that are promised to

Christians who help the poor.   Here are two examples:

- He who has pity on the poor lends to the Lord, and He will pay back what he has given. Proverbs 19:17

- Blessed is he who considers the poor; The Lord will deliver him in time of trouble. The Lord will preserve him and keep him alive, and he will be blessed on the earth. You will not deliver him to the will of his enemies. The Lord will strengthen him on his bed of illness. You will sustain him on his sickbed. Psalm 41:1-3

I believe God also wants us to pay special attention to the poor, especially those who are brothers and sisters in Christ, and those who are members of our biological family. I have watched people who claim to be Christians ignore the financial needs of their own immediate family members.   I have noticed that Christians who are able to help the poor but don't, often end up having both financial and health issues. I believe that where God makes a promise there is also a warning. Consider the poor and God will cause you to be blessed, but ignore the poor and God may remove your blessing.

Perhaps because I didn't grow up in a well off family I've always had a tremendous amount of compassion for the poor.   I'm always a sucker for people who stand next to street intersections with signs asking for money. I know that some of them will spend the money on alcohol or drugs, but some are simply in a bad place and need help. The bottom line is that both our country and the world are full of people who are poor. God puts these people in our lives for a reason. If we have the means to help them and we ignore them, we are breaking God's law. The Bible says in James 4:17, "To him who knows to do good and does not do it, to him it is sin."

So while this not-so-secret formula is available to all of us, many Believers find it so very difficult to follow. I encourage you to put God to the test in this area of your life. You'll be amazed by what He will do!

THIRTY TWO

Which Are You?

There are only two types of people in the world, so there are only two types of people who will ever read this book: those who have said "yes" to Jesus and those who have not. There's no middle ground. For those who know Jesus personally this book will be a huge encouragement to you. It will cause you to remember all of the amazing miracles God has done in your life. This book could have been written by you, with just as many examples of how God came to your rescue in an unexpected way and at an unexpected time.

I can think of so many examples I've heard over the years from other Christians, like my small group Bible study friend named Tom. Early in his marriage he and his wife were struggling financially. They reached a point where they didn't have any money for groceries. They had a large coin jar and decided to begin rolling coins to use for groceries. About half way through the jar they found a $100 dollar bill in the middle of the jar! Neither of them had put it in there!

Then there are those who have not said yes to Jesus, or they think they are Christians but are not. They are "religious" but have never made Jesus the "Savior and Lord" of their lives. Quite honestly I'm not sure what you'll think of a book like this one. Perhaps you'll think I made all this up. I didn't. Everything written here is true. In fact there are many more miracles I could have included in this book. My hope it that you'll begin to see how incredibly loving God really is.

Some skeptics will read this book and say "So what. I found five bucks in a parking lot last summer and I was sick once and got better." Remember the math I did on the quarters I found for the parking meter. A very conservative estimate put the odds of that happening at 1 in 500,000. So think about the odds of several dozen statistically improbable events happening in one person's life. The rule of compound probability that applied to tossing one coin several times also applies here. One or two miraculous events in one person's life might be explained away, but not dozens.

The Bible says that "God demonstrates His love for us in that while we were yet sinners, Christ died for us". The Bible says that "God so loved the world, that He gave His only Begotten Son, that whosoever believes in Him shall not perish but have everlasting life." My hope is that today you will say yes to Jesus. He is the answer to every question you have in life.

THIRTY THREE

Closing Thoughts

I have a theory and my guess is that it's probably not a widely held belief. My theory stems from a belief held by an amazing Bible scholar named Dr. Chuck Missler. Dr. Missler believes that everything in the Bible, every date, every name, etc. is there by design and has meaning. He provides overwhelming evidence for his belief in his extensive and detailed Bible commentaries.

For example, in the Old Testament book of numbers we read an account of the size of each of the 12 tribes of Israel and how they arranged themselves while they camped in the wilderness. On the surface it seems like an insignificant piece of information. However, Dr. Missler discovered that when you arrange them just as described in the Bible, they form the shape of a cross. This shouldn't surprise us. Remember what Jesus said to the Pharisees: "You search the Scriptures (the Old Testament), for in them you think you have eternal life; and these are they which testify of Me" John 5:39.

So my theory, which is related to this belief by Dr. Missler, is that every detail **in our lives as Christians** is there by design. Every person you meet, every trial you encounter, the people you work with and for, your neighbors, none of these things are just there by coincidence. God is intimately involved in the lives of His children. The problem is that we are so busy building "our" kingdom that we miss out on opportunities to build "His" kingdom. How many opportunities to do good works did God give me over the years that I missed because I wasn't paying attention? Many thousands I'm sure.

In early April 2002, three different employees from my office approached me at work wanting to know more about my faith. Two of them basically told me that their lives were a disaster and they wanted to know more about what I believed. At that point in time I had worked in this particular office for several years and never had anything like this happen, especially not three times in one week. Well the very next week, I was laid off and never saw any of them again. God knew what was just around the corner and He gave me one last opportunity to be a witness for Him in my office. What seemed like a strange coincidence to me at the time was anything but that.

In the summer of 2006 while we were living in Cincinnati, a vacant parcel of land right near our home caught my attention. It was on the corner of a new shopping center that included a Kroger and a Panera Bread. Ever since I had arrived in Cincinnati I was frustrated that there were no decent car washes in the city. This small corner property looked just perfect for a new car wash. Even though the idea sounded crazy to me, I went online and found a "how to" book on opening and running a car wash and began reading.

When I called the property owner he said that more than a dozen people had already called him about putting a car wash on that very spot. I was on to something. The problem in my mind was that I had spent my entire career in an office setting. Even though I have always had a very entrepreneurial side to me a car wash was way outside my comfort zone. Just as I was finishing the "how to" book I had purchased I met the father of one of Lauren's classmates. It turned out that he was managing a car wash located just a few minutes from our home.

So you would think that the next thing I would have done was share my "crazy" idea with him about building a car wash in my neighborhood. But I didn't. The idea sounded so crazy to me that I thought it couldn't be something God wanted me to do. Six months later I lost my job and we then moved a few months after that to Dallas. My best guess is that this was God's plan for how we could have stayed in Cincinnati. But I didn't pursue it.

A few months after I abandoned my idea one of the largest companies in the U.S. purchased the lot and built a beautiful three million dollar car wash on the site. This location was their pilot for what has become a nationwide chain of Mr. Clean car washes. Clearly I was on to something, and God was up to something. I missed my chance.

When things happen to you in your Christian life that are unusual and you start to think it's only a coincidence, think again. If my theory is right, there is no such thing as a coincidence for those of us who truly know Jesus. If you think God might be leading you in a particular direction take a small step or two and see what happens. If it is truly from God then He will continue to open doors for you and if you stick with it, amazing things will happen.

When some of the events detailed in this book occurred in my life, I felt they were just random occurrences or just plain bad luck. I didn't understand until much later that, in each case, God was working out a specific plan. My writing this first book is of course not just some random thing that I decided to do. My guess is that this will lead me in some new direction. I have no idea what's around the corner but I know that God has a plan and a purpose in this. In fact, I already know the second book I am supposed to write. And I'm sure that this time around, I won't wait a full year to get started.

Lauren, Ryan and Hannah, I don't know what impact this book will have on you in the coming years. I honestly didn't think I would actually write it. I never thought I would find the time or the words. But God kept prompting me to continue. He kept giving me ideas for what to include.

As I was getting close the finishing this book I asked my wife Cathy and my oldest daughter Lauren to read the manuscript and give me their feedback. They both felt that not many people other than friends and family would want to read this book. They gave me this feedback on a Tuesday and I got a little depressed about it. Maybe they were right. Perhaps my story was something that complete strangers would have no interest in reading.

On Saturday of that same week I printed out the lesson plan for Sunday school. Cathy and I both teach 1st grade Sunday school and each month we receive a new lesson plan. At the beginning of each plan is the new "bottom line" for that month's lesson. There at the top of the page was the new bottom line and it read "Jesus wants to use your story to make a difference." Once again God was telling me to "keep writing".

I want to close this book with a reminder to Lauren, Ryan and Hannah that we live in a fallen world, a world that is marred by the effects of sin. The account of man's fall is found in Genesis chapter three. The resulting "curse" affects creation, relationships, childbearing and even work. Because of this the three of you will be afflicted throughout your lives with various trials and incredibly difficult situations. This world will break your hearts. But remember that if you commit your way to God, He will direct your paths. He will work all things together for good. Remember that "many are the afflictions of the righteous, but the Lord delivers him out of them all."

I want to believe that all three of you will continue attending a good Bible teaching church when you leave home. I want to believe that you will live your lives in obedience to God's Word. But I know the math is against me on this. The math suggests that you won't all make it.

The most recent book I read was "No Easy Day", a first-hand account by a Navy Seal of the killing of Osama Bin Laden. From the heavy profanity used throughout the book it was clear to me that the author was not a Believer. But what I discovered in reading the book was that his parents were not only Christians, but missionaries in Alaska. It's so depressing to see this but it happens all too often today. So if there is one more miracle I would ask of God, it is that the three of you will "beat the odds" and all make it into Heaven one day.

Second John 1:4 says "I have no greater joy than to know my children walk in the truth." This book is full of truth, not my truth but God's truth. You each have a choice to make. You can choose to walk in the truth or to live your lives apart from God. I have spent one half of my life without God and the other half walking in the truth.

I can tell you from personal experience that the life God has for you is an abundant life. I can also tell you that life apart for Him is empty and unsatisfying. I want to remind you that God doesn't have any grandchildren. You won't make it into Heaven simply because your mom and I will be there. You have to make your own decision for Jesus. All I can do is point you in the right direction.

And please don't make the mistake I made on more than one occasion of focusing on "people" rather than on Jesus. All people, even true Christians, make mistakes. They still sin. Don't anchor your life to or place your hope in people, anchor your life to Jesus and to the promises He has given you in the Bible. Don't let hypocrisy by people who claim to be Christians derail your faith. I did this in high school and as a result wasted 10 years of my life.

My final thought is that God loves each of you more than you could ever think or imagine. He watches over the smallest details of our lives, even things we would consider to be insignificant. Even when we don't feel that He is close to us, He is. He's right there through every trial and challenge. He never leaves us. The miracles He does in our lives are evidence of His love for us.

It has been said that you'll never know that Jesus is all you need until Jesus is all you have. Please believe me when I tell you that Jesus is all you'll ever need.

www.ingramcontent.com/pod-product-compliance
Lightning Source LLC
Chambersburg PA
CBHW060927040426

42445CB00011B/836